D1226385

HOW TO KEEP
DINOSAURS

Robert Mash, M.A.(Hons), B.Sc., M.I.Biol., was born in 1939. He read zoology at Oxford University, where he was Walter Galpin Scholar of Balliol College, and researched gull behaviour there with Nobel Laureate Professor Niko Tinbergen, F.R.S. Mr Mash was at that time a Scientific Fellow of the Zoological Society of London, a member of the Association for the Study of Animal Behaviour, and a member of the Mammal Society of the British Isles, and he wrote regularly for the magazine *Animals*. After leaving Oxford he became a Senior Programmer with Educational Systems Ltd and wrote several texts, including *Sterilization Techniques for Nurses, Solutions and Crystallisation, Clostridial Sheep Diseases* and *Cervical Cytology*. In 1968 he joined the Department of Audio-Visual Communication of the British Medical Association as Research Officer. Since 1969 Robert Mash has been head of the biology department at Clayesmore School. He lives in a thatched cottage in the middle of Dorset which he, his wife and his son share with orchids, chameleons, crickets, and an owl and a pussycat.

·HOW TO KEEP·
DINOSAURS

ROBERT MASH

ILLUSTRATED BY
·WILLIAM RUSHTON·
PHILIP HOOD · DIZ WALLIS

ANDRE DEUTSCH

Deinonychus, a potential aid to police forces and generals. For care and feeding, see page 29.

CONTENTS

INTRODUCTION

I intend this book mainly as a help to average pet lovers who wish to keep a dinosaur or two in their house or garden. I also talk about some species that are best left, perhaps, to large land-owners who already have some experience of keeping animals that need a lot of space. I shall show you that, whereas the dinosaurs with which you may already be familiar are monumentally huge, there are many, many species that are small and manageable enough to be kept successfully as pets, and many that are ideal for farming and other purposes. The book deals with most of the better-known dinosaurs, and is intended to encourage the beginner.

What is a dinosaur?

Times change, and with them people's ideas of dinosaurs. The animals included here form a natural group, at least in the opinion of many experts. This may be called the Superclass Endosauropsida, and includes not only the dinosaurs proper but also the flying forms known as pterosaurs. A simple classification of the Endosauropsida may be found on page 70.

This Superclass Endosauropsida contains as varied a group of animals as can be imagined. They range in size from the sparrow-like *Pterodactylus* to *Brachiosaurus* (eighty tons) and *Diplodocus* (eighty-five feet). There are stupid ones like *Stegosaurus* and intelligent ones like *Deinonychus*. Some, like *Iguanodon,* are vegetarian; others, like *Ceratosaurus,* are carnivorous. The brontosaurs are ponderous and slow, but *Struthiomimus* can race along at 50 mph. *Pteranodon* is covered in fur, *Archaeopteryx* in feathers, *Polacanthus* in spines and *Nodosaurus* in warts. *Anatosaurus* is mild and gentle; *Tyrannosaurus* is lethal.

Why keep dinosaurs?

As you can see, the dinosaurs (or endosauropsids, to be strictly accurate) are a fascinatingly varied group of animals. I cannot recommend the largest as domestic pets, but the small ones, particularly the pseudo-suchians and coelurosaurs, will fit perfectly into any home as long as the owner takes a few elementary precautions. Many of them require no special housing and can live on household scraps; others can be trained as guard "dogs" and can be of great use to security organizations and the police. Indeed, the most imaginative of military experts can see their limited deployment as tactical weapons of war, particularly in tropical climates. A further attraction of the dinosaurs is that, in these conservation-conscious days, the keeping of rare or threatened species is rightly frowned upon by ecologists: no qualms of this kind can hinder the dinosaur-keeper, who deals only with animals that are already extinct.

What should the beginner start with? If you are familiar with dinosaurs, you may be surprised to see the pseudosuchians in my classification; you naturally expect to see this attractive group tucked away as a suborder of the Thecodonta. I cannot here go into the reasons for removing the warm-blooded, active, bipedal pseudosuchians from the cold-blooded, semi-static, quadrupedal, reptilian thecodonts, beyond saying that there are good ones. For practical reasons, there is nothing better for beginners to cut their teeth on than a pseudosuchian such as *Euparkeria*.

The long names may be a snag to start with. I believe, however, that dinosaur-keepers in most cases prefer the name, like the animal, to be long and antique.

DINOSAURS for BEGINNERS

Order Pseudosuchia
PODOPTERYX

A gliding conversation piece, and a perfect first dinosaur. A cage in a warm room and the usual cat foods are all that Podopteryx needs, and in summer it can go outdoors.

P odopteryx is, of course, a true pseudosuchian and not to be confused with the Miocene scorpaenoid acanthopterygian of the same name. It is in fact a small gliding dinosaur with a thin membrane of skin stretching from knees to elbows and from ankles to tail. Stability is maintained by means of the long tail stretching out behind. The hind legs are the most important limbs for controlling gliding and, as the membrane is elastic, *Podopteryx* has a fairly controlled "flight", rather like that of Leadbeater's Possum *(Gymnobelideus)*. Also like that marsupial, it cannot "flap" its "wings" and "fly" properly: it must glide down from a higher point to a lower one.

Podopteryx is omnivorous, with a preference for animal matter; cat-foods are usually taken, dog-foods are often rejected. It is a lovable creature and easily kept. You should provide it with an enclosure wired in on all sides and on top; remember it is a climber and can easily glide out if you have no roof. Give it shrubs, or better still, a tree or two to climb about in, though if too many tall trees are provided you may never see this charming but shy creature as it hides in the foliage. It prefers deciduous trees. This is curious, as these are not to be found on the North side of the Himalayas in the Soviet Kirgizstan Triassic, where *Podopteryx* was first discovered in 1970.

You can allow your *Podopteryx* the freedom of most rooms in the house. It will have a natural inclination to climb any convenient drapes or curtains and to float

spectacularly down at its leisure. Since it does not flap its "wings", the gliding process is completely silent. It is, therefore, as well to warn visitors – especially elderly relatives and nervous individuals – of its presence, as tame specimens love to alight on the shoulders, or sometimes the heads, of anyone passing by.

Although shy by nature, *Podopteryx* – particularly those kept singly – grow to adore human company and can become extremely affectionate. They enjoy being stroked and will sit on your shoulders for hours if permitted. In fact, it can sometimes be quite difficult to get them off; if they cannot be tempted away by food, there are two other ruses which generally work. One is to climb to the top of a very tall tree and then begin to climb down again; at this point *Podopteryx* will realize that he is in danger of missing the opportunity for an especially lengthy and satisfying glide and will gently disengage and float away. It is then imperative to stay in the tree until your pet has landed either on the ground or on someone else, for if you come down too quickly *Podopteryx* may make a slow circular descent, carefully timed to coincide with your own return to ground level. Athletic owners may at first find this an amusing game and source of exercise, but it is definitely not to be encouraged.

The alternative is to invest in a dressmaker's dummy or a store-window type mannequin and always to wear a jacket which you don't mind taking off and leaving.

Order Pseudosuchia
EUPARKERIA

For the beginner, or experienced reptile-keeper, the classical first step on the romantic road of dinosaur keeping. Warm-blooded, active, small, manageable, and easily fed on scraps.

I f you are used to keeping reptiles such as iguanas, you should definitely start your dinosaur collection with a pseudosuchian, and I warmly recommend *Euparkeria* as an alternative to *Podopteryx* (page 7). The pseudosuchians mark a border line between reptiles and dinosaurs. Their principal virtue is their relatively small size and consequent manageability. They are mostly naked, without fur or feathers and therefore need fairly warm quarters. Like the other dinosaurs, they are warm-blooded and active.

Euparkeria is about three feet long and to most tastes an attractive animal, although – like many objects of enduring appeal – it may take some getting used to. Your first sight of an *Euparkeria* will almost certainly be when it is resting or walking on all fours, when its legs are spread out sideways like a lizard's; however, once the creature is running, its hind legs

move under the body to give it that speed and support which is so much a part of their function. In other respects *Euparkeria* looks not unlike an iguana. There is a curious lump between the front of the head and the eyes which contains what seems to be some sort of gland. It is not yet known what this is for, so there is an opportunity here for amateur natural historians to undertake some research! Indeed, ambitious parents will appreciate that, in an age when opportunities for this type of really useful research are increasingly hard to find, a child who grows up with *Euparkeria* in the house may well be on a winner when the time for doctoral theses comes around.

Like *Podopteryx, Euparkeria* grow to be affectionate and keen on company. They love to be patted and stroked, especially with a fingernail drawn sensuously back from the tip of the nose, across the forehead and skull, and on down to the nape of the neck. Two minutes of this makes them positively glow with satisfaction and take on a facial expression which some fanciers describe as "smiling". Sadly, this is a euphemism. The "smile" of the hyper-contented *Euparkeria* closely resembles the anticipatory leer of the human psychopath: the hooded eyelids droop rendering the eyes barely visible, the upper lips retract revealing the pointed teeth, the jaw drops open and the tongue lolls from side to side.

The uninitiated should not be introduced to a *Euparkeria* in this state. However, the facial expressions of this lovable pseudosuchian, like those of Presidents and Prime Ministers, are another aspect of the creature which its supporters quickly get used to.

Euparkeria is a true carnivore, and most individuals must have a diet consisting largely of cold meat.

Euparkeria is lovable and full of mischief. Take care when there's food about.

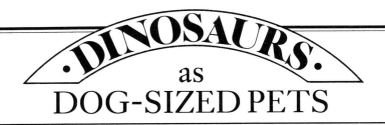

· DINOSAURS · as
DOG-SIZED PETS

Suborder Sauropodomorpha
THECODONTOSAURUS

An underestimated small prosauropod with all the desirable dinosaurian qualities and none of the inconveniences. Large enough to impress your neighbours but small enough to be manageable.

Most of this animal's ten-foot length is tail and much of the rest is neck. Its shape is almost classically brontosaurian but without the exuberance that spoils so many of those large vegetarians. It is normally a quadruped but can also stand on its hind legs and even walk on them.

Although it is mainly carnivorous, *Thecodontosaurus* has a liking for plant food. Give it mainly meat: dog food with plenty of green or root vegetables will do. In summer, it can stay outside in a large garden or paddock. In winter give it a spare room or a heated outhouse, and exercise it every day. It enjoys walking and runs in an unusual, very flat-footed manner, faintly reminiscent of Oliver Hardy hurrying on all fours. It is certainly advisable to keep it on a lead in towns, and probably at all times because it is liable to get lost and indeed – due to its extremely short memory – to forget who its owner is. It is a good pet for joggers, who should acquire a long elasticated leash, and a very fit specimen is an undoubted asset to publicity conscious marathon runners. It is frankly rather a stupid animal, and you will not be able to train it to do anything useful. Concentrate on getting it to remember its own name, which should be as short as possible, such as "Ay", "You", or "Ron". It is affectionate, good with children and, for a dinosaur, easy to manage.

Suborder Ornithopoda
FABROSAURUS

Undemanding and amiable, Fabrosaurus is easily fed and will live happily in the house during the winter, and with your goats in the garden during the summer.

Fabrosaurus is about three feet long and has long, slender back legs: it is, in fact, mainly bipedal and a good runner. It has a horny beak which it uses for cropping tough plants. It is very undemanding and loves to chew anything. Think of it as a little goat, although, unlike a goat, *Fabrosaurus* has no pelt, and so needs heated quarters in winter. It will live contentedly enough in the house, although no one has managed to house-train it. Try wiring off a corner of the kitchen right up to the ceiling, because *Fabrosaurus* can climb! It is sure-footed and has stamina, and is therefore especially recommended for hikers and cross-country walkers. In all a fairly amiable little beast, but not very bright: in fact, pretty dull, but room may be found in most households for fancied individuals.

Suborder Ornithopoda
STEGOCERAS

For the person who would like a friendly and inoffensive pet, pretty and easily fed, Stegoceras is ideal as long as its feet are not allowed to stay wet.

When fully grown these pretty creatures are generally about the height of a man. They are also bipedal and pleasingly sociable. They therefore make most interesting pets because they can walk along beside you on approximately equal terms. Moreover, they will not demur at the idea of holding hands. They are especially recommended for lonely people; and there is an opportunity here for the imaginative entrepreneur: breed yourself a flock, take the prettiest one with you and collect orders from the unfortunates who come out of singles bars on their own.

Of all the dinosaurs *Stegoceras* is perhaps most likely to become in time *the* smart pet. It is, after all, much more interesting than either an alligator or a chihuahua, and even cheetahs will soon be old hat. Of course, if this happens, there is a danger that the smart set will want to put clothes on them and take them around in private jets. I have no evidence, but I feel this might be a little much for *Stegoceras* and could lead to neurosis and the whole gamut of anxiety-induced illnesses. It could provoke a regression to the wild state, even in those bred in domesticity. A non-house-trained *Stegoceras* would retain very little chic.

We must not forget that, despite its humanoid stance, *Stegoceras* is a bone-headed dinosaur, physi-

cally and figuratively. The five-inch-thick dome of solid bone at the top of the head protects a brain not much more than two inches long. There is an attractive bony frill at the back of the head.

As far as feeding is concerned, think of *Stegoceras* as a sheep that doesn't eat grass but eats everything else that a sheep eats. As far as accommodation is concerned, think of *Stegoceras* as a sheep without wool: be sure to keep it warm!

Their feet must be kept dry, or they are very likely to catch cold. Look carefully for any slightly unusual behaviour patterns such as shivering or unexpected vertical jumps. The most immediate cure is to swab the throat with eucalyptus. You may notice one day that your otherwise not unduly lascivious *Stegoceras* is persistently winking at you. Fortunately, this does not presage what it seems. It is merely the onset of a disease, peculiar to *Stegoceras* and some other dinosaurs, known as "one-eyed cold", the symptom of which is the frequent and rather saucy closing of one eye. Isolate the dinosaur and cure with heat treatment. This is also good for dinosaur asthma which occasionally attacks the more sensitive and less intelligent herbivores such as *Stegoceras*, particularly when they have experienced difficulty in making a decision. Do not therefore give them a choice of foods.

A male *Heterodontosaurus* warding off a rival. Note the breeder's protective legwear.

Suborder Ornithopoda
HETERODONTOSAURUS

A very interesting, lively, and easily satisfied dinosaur, Heterodontosaurus is affectionate and well-disposed. It is often called the rich man's Fabrosaurus. It can easily become part of the family.

H eterodontosaurus is about three feet long and, unless it's in a hurry, it goes around on all fours. It is herbivorous and easily satisfied. As far as food goes, it is like *Fabrosaurus:* if a goat will eat it, so will *Heterodontosaurus*. In addition, *Heterodontosaurus* has no problems with honeysuckle. It is similar to *Fabrosaurus* in many other ways, although more delicate and, one must add, much more of a nuisance. Its grasping hands and grasping feet tend to clutch anything within reach in the home: this makes it more interesting to visitors than to owners.

It is, however, affectionate as well as lively. Children love to cuddle it, and there is no reason why they shouldn't as long as they don't mind being licked in return. The end of a child's bed is as good a place for the creature to sleep as any. *Heterodontosaurus* is fascinated by television, and this is a sure way to create a hiatus in its incessant picking up and dropping of valuable objects. It is totally transfixed by all sport and much comedy (try it on *Barney Miller*), and will snuggle down goggle-eyed with child or adult.

The male is a bit of a handful at mating time and may need to be kept under firm control. Although he is usually of a mild disposition, he will unhesitatingly use his "canines" to attack rivals; and as he is not good at telling the difference between rivals and other moving objects, he may well wound female and owner alike in his vague but intense sexual aggressive frenzy. If you are a serious breeder, you will find that some form of leg protection is useful: spats, gaiters, baseball or cricket pads – assemble whatever you can. Equipment for dinosaur enthusiasts may soon become big business; one of the first items on sale will be protective leggings for *Heterodontosaurus* breeders.

Suborder Ceratopia
LEPTOCERATOPS

If you have a small paddock, Leptoceratops is a very feasible ceratopian for you. It is easily fed and housed – and suited to captivity.

L eptoceratops is about six feet long, and unlike the other members of the suborder Ceratopia – the Horned Dinosaurs – it is unhorned, a biped and an agile runner. *Leptoceratops* is tricky to tame and impossible to house-train. A muzzle is recommended when bringing them into the house, which is not itself recommended unless the furniture is screwed to the floor. Mature females may become sufficiently fond of their owners to render these precautions either unnecessary or extremely necessary.

It is essential to provide half an acre or so of land for the creature, because it requires fresh vegetation, and, like penurious *literati*, is happiest when browsing. It prefers slightly softer food than its larger relatives, but will accept much the same diet as recommended for them (see *Triceratops*, page 54). No one, as far as I have been able to discover, has bred these creatures. As a consequence, they are in fairly short supply. This is a pity as it means that many prospective owners turn to the easier, but less interesting, *Protoceratops*.

as
LAP PETS

Suborder Theropoda
PODOKESAURUS

A pretty little theropod, easily fed and good with children. A centrally-heated apartment should suit it well, with the use of a garden in summer.

This pleasant little theropod is a smaller form of *Coelophysis* (page 27) and is only about three feet long. It is lightly built and runs around quickly on its hind limbs. It is very pretty and an attractive green colour. It loves playing with children and is very manageable. It is carnivorous and you should give it a good commercial dog-food, preferably of the type that has largish chunks of good red meat in it. Better still, feed *Podokesaurus* daily on live cockroaches, crickets, locusts (very useful), rhinoceros beetles and mealworms. This base should be supplemented with live mice and small birds to provide exercise, calcium and roughage. *Podokesaurus* needs warmed quarters in winter. Keep it inside if there is an R in the month. Otherwise you may find it a martyr to coughs and sneezes.

Now is a good time to buy *Podokesaurus*: they can be picked up at huge discounts and even "two for the price of one", which is well worth considering. The glut has been caused by demand in Britain, formerly a major consumer, dropping to almost zero. *Podokesaurus* comes from the Middle Triassic of Argentina.

Suborder Theropoda
MICROVENATOR

A tameable, trainable, lovable and easy-to-feed dromaeosaur, easily kept in a centrally-heated apartment where its small size and ready intelligence make it a safe pet for children.

Microvenator is the smallest of the dromaeosaurs (or deinonychosaurs, as some people prefer to call them). The dromaeosaurs are the unexpected dinosaurs: they are small (relatively), nimble, speedy, and intelligent; they need no massive cages or paddocks; they are basically ferocious but tameable and even trainable; they are lovable and easily, though not cheaply, fed. They are dinosaurs for the common man. Some, like cats, are nocturnal but, unlike cats, they should not be put out at night as they will eat cats, not to mention dogs.

Children adore *Microvenator* and it adores them, liking nothing better than to be hugged, squeezed, carried, put to bed, pushed around on tricycles and to join in any fun that's going. *Microvenator* also makes a very suitable lap pet for the increasing numbers of adults who have nothing better to do than sit around with dinosaurs on their laps. *Microvenator* usually catches its food with outstretched hands. In captivity it will catch dog foods thrown gently toward it.

Suborder Theropoda
COMPSOGNATHUS

Perfect for city dwellers, chicken-sized, gentle, loving and easily house-trained and fine with children. Should suit small family in a centrally-heated apartment.

About a foot long, with feathers and grasping fingers. Like so many coelurosaurs, *Compsognathus* has hollow bones filled with air so that it is very light and extremely agile. There are several species, and colours vary one to another, tending towards the gaudy, with oranges and blues predominating.

Compsognathus is the ideal dinosaur for city dwellers. It is hardy and adaptable. Once it learns to recognize its owner, it is mild-mannered and affectionate. It is small enough to share an apartment or a small house, and if encouraged right from birth can often be house-trained, especially if induced to use its own lavatory area. It is perfectly safe with children, but its grasping fingers are often a nuisance in well-furnished houses, so that a certain degree of confinement may be appropriate.

Compsognathus is carnivorous, feeding on mammals, lizards, insects, small pterosaurs – anything it can get its hands on. It prefers its food alive, and specimens provided with an animate diet prosper more, and are more likely to breed, than those brought up on scraps and corpses. Breeding is no problem so long as the couple is given a measure of privacy.

Temperature is a releaser of breeding behaviour in *Compsognathus*. If your dinosaurs steadfastly refuse to copulate (in hard cases, even to court), raising of the temperature by 5°F will often do the trick; if not, spraying the animal with warm water may work. Try them both (raised temperature and spray) together.

Space is needed by dinosaurs just as much as time is needed by Englishmen: stubbornly infertile females become fecund and males make fresh efforts when extra acres are added to their playgrounds.

Feeding may be crucial. I advise a high protein diet before breeding. Do not let males eat too much food: too much starch and not enough exercise fattens them so that copulation may become difficult, or even impossible.

The period of laying and incubation is always difficult. Give the females as much isolation and quiet as possible and keep the males away. Disturb the sitting dinosaurs as little as you can: the more disturbance, the greater the likelihood of eggs being trodden on.

Compsognathus corallestris is an aquatic form in which the fingers are no longer separate but joined to make paddles. It is a swimmer and diver, blackish in colour and hugely entertaining. It eats seafood and is keen on crustacea: scampi and lobster suit it best.

It is more difficult to keep satisfactorily than its land-based relations, but a bathroom converted into a cage will work very well.

·DINOSAURS·
as
FLYING PETS

Order Aves
ARCHAEOPTERYX

The first bird! Easily kept, fed and bred, there is an Archaeopteryx for every occasion. Choose a species to suit your home and pocket.

Dinosaur systematists will insist, and not without reason, that *Archaeopteryx* is a bird. However, it is better, in what is essentially a practical manual, to put it among its close relatives. If you wish to think of it as a bird, do so: both authority and common sense are on your side. Perhaps only pedants and romantics would really wish to stress its ancestry in preference to its vulgar relations.

Archaeopteryx is our smallest dinosaur, weighing only about one pound. It is, in appearance, a typical small coelurosaur, but covered in feathers like a bird. Like all coelurosaurs it has well-developed teeth, a long tail and grasping hands; like most birds it has feathers all over its body, in two rows along the sides of its tail and a typically avian arrangement of ten primary feathers and fourteen secondaries on its arms. It moults twice a year and in all species the male is much more brightly coloured than the drab female. Species differ in colour and pattern; pay your money and take your choice. It can fly, of course.

Treated well, *Archaeopteryx* can become quite tame and affectionate. Although it should live out of doors in an aviary, it will enjoy being brought into the house from time to time. If you want to see a lot of your *Archaeopteryx,* build the aviary on to your house so that your pets can join you in your living quarters whenever they wish. *Archaeopteryx* is generally well-behaved in the presence of humans. The squawk of most species is somewhat reminiscent of a chair being

dragged across a stone floor. If this irritates, use ear muffs or a Walkman radio. Its teeth are very sharp, so whatever you do, don't annoy it. In fact, it is a good idea to let it have its own way at all times, and to be as subservient as possible. Get up if it wants to sit in your chair, turn up the heating when it is moulting, even though this will be in mid-summer and, ideally, keep a dish of live mice on the coffee table so that *Archaeopteryx* can have a snack whenever it feels like one. Living with *Archaeopteryx* is good for those with over-inflated egos, and they therefore make good presents for film stars, talk show hosts, astronauts and the like.

Different species prefer different food; in general try live food or recently dead. Day-old chicks, dragonflies, white mice and cat-food are good basic stand-bys. Some individuals of at least two species love peanuts, almost to distraction. Juniper berries are not without impact, particularly to courting couples, although, if given to ovulating females, may cause the eggs to be addled.

As you can see, *Archaeopteryx* is a carnivore: in the wild it feeds on insects, lizards, small mammals, and so on. Like most perching birds, it catches its food in its bill. Disregard what you may read about its hands being used to grasp the prey and the feathers helping in the capture of it. The authors of such books and articles have clearly never seen *Archaeopteryx* feeding. I accept that it does use its hands for grasping branches and leaves, and I will not rule out the possibility that in one species, the Black Archaeopteryx, its

Archaeopteryx is highly decorative, and well behaved as long as you pamper him thoroughly.

hands may be used to sift through the undergrowth for food, though I have never seen this. However, *I have on no occasion seen* Archaeopteryx *transfer edible material to its mouth with its hands.* Nor do I believe that anyone else has.

In spite of what so many books – particularly new ones – say, *Archaeopteryx* is able to fly, though not very strongly and not for long distances. Taking off from a level surface always presents difficulties. Fortunately the claws on its wings, at the wrist, allow it to scramble up trees. Provide it, therefore, with shrubs and sticks to climb.

In fact, *Archaeopteryx* has many types of feeding behaviour, and the food you give a particular species should be related as closely as possible to this behaviour. For example, the Black Archaeopteryx, which has marvellous golden legs, likes to leap into leaf litter and loose undergrowth, where it scrabbles backwards with its feet (with its arms as well, according to some accounts). This disturbs or reveals the prey which can then be pecked up by the beak. Give this species, then, the sorts of things you find in undergrowth. Another species, the Melodious Archaeopteryx (song simple but pleasing) eats molluscs. The Rough-legged Archaeopteryx, parachutes from trees on to its prey of shrews and rodents. The Small-eared Archaeopteryx has large eyes and big ears. It is nocturnal and so is its prey: give it plenty of night life.

Breeding is not only feasible but likely. Most species will pair up naturally if kept in fairly large groups. When such a pair seems to have formed, remove it to a separate breeding enclosure. Here, if you leave them as undisturbed as you can, they may mate. The cock will display his tail (and in some species his brightly-coloured teeth) and neck-feathers to the hen and sing. This sound, usually raucous, repetitive and unpleasing to our ears, seems to unlock the hen's hitherto undisclosed longing: she will then respond, coyly but unmistakeably, to his advances. Such increased amorous susceptibility is temporary and brief at first, and at this stage the female will flee if the male progresses too quickly from the oral to the tactile; she may well bite irritatingly persistent males. However, as his song stokes up her amatory fire, she will become increasingly receptive to his more palpable approaches and eventually union is consummated. Up to a dozen eggs (thirteen in the so-called *A. boulangeria*) are soon laid in a primitive nest in a tree. These hatch in three to four weeks, depending on the species. The naked chicks are incubated by the hen until they get their own feathers about ten days later. At this stage they are at their most vulnerable: if the hen leaves the nest for too long, the nestlings may catch cold and die, particularly in cold weather. Don't disturb her at this period. Mother and chicks are fed by father. A week or more after fledging, the young are pecking at more or less everything that moves, and are capable of catching the odd insect. From then on they become more and more self-reliant and independent. If the eggs are soft-shelled this may be due to a deficiency of lime in the mother's diet: next time add lime to her food. However, it may be due to nervous shock: if *you* are not responsible, ten to one her partner started singing at an inappropriate moment. Try to teach him that timing is everything – by example.

Class Pterosauria

THE PTEROSAURS

*A fascinating and, for the most part, attractive group of airborne creatures,
many of whom make charming family pets.*

Y es, I know that pterosaurs are not dinosaurs, but they are endosauropsids and as such they are associated in the popular mind with dinosaurs, and any book on dinosaur husbandry *must* cover the pterosaurs.

I shall describe the pterosaurs as a group here and now. The peculiarities of individual species are described under separate headings.

Housing

Shelters should be at least as long and wide as they are high, because pterosaurs do not find it very easy to fly straight upward. There is a danger that they might fall to the floor and be unable to regain their perches. If the shelter is open-fronted, no windows are needed; if it can be completely closed in, at least one window (not clear glass, because they will fly into it) should be built into one of the sides to allow in plenty of light. Otherwise the pterosaurs might not use the shelter and be difficult to drive in at night.

The framework of the outdoor part of the cage can be of sawed timber but rustic poles look much nicer and blend better with the garden surroundings. Sawn timber will have to be painted or creosoted at regular intervals to preserve it, whereas rustic poles (so I'm told) need no maintenance.

Some pterosaurs spend a great deal of their time in the air or in the water, but even these may like to roost in trees at night. Other pterosaurs perch or hang up a great deal. It is important, therefore, that perches should be of the right thickness – about that of a pencil for *Pterodactylus elegans,* and up to broom handle width and more for larger species. A perch should be too thin rather than too thick – something for them to get their claws round. Natural tree branches are best, although machine-made dowelling is quite satisfactory. Perches should be firmly fixed for the larger species for two reasons: they do not like alighting on swaying twigs; and they cannot cling at steep angles, unlike perching birds. Fix perches at each end of the aviary to give the pterosaurs maximum flying space.

Pterosaurs do not thrive in cages. They are reduced to immobility by close confinement and become uninteresting. Moreover, one of their greatest attractions – their sleek, glossy pelage – is lost under indoor conditions unless they are regularly sprayed with water and given bathing facilities.

Characteristics

All pterosaurs are warm-blooded and most are furred. Many have teeth, though some have lost them. Their most obvious characteristic is the membrane (usually fur-covered) that extends from the front arms, particularly the enormously lengthened ring finger, to the knees, or, in some cases, ankles. This is used for flight like the membrane of a bat's wing. To make the animal lighter, the bones are filled with air, as are those of birds.

As in birds, sight is good and smell commonly poor. Unlike most birds (except the crows and parrots) they are markedly intelligent and in most cases perfectly trainable. Only *Sordes* sets its mind firmly against personal cleanliness. It should be possible to breed all the smaller pterosaurs, but the small long-tailed ones still prove obdurate and the largest short-tailed ones are still pretty tricky.

As a general rule, the short-tailed pterosaurs make more satisfactory pets than the long-tailed ones: they are more intelligent, cleaner, better-looking and less delicate.

Sordes is charming but somewhat unhygienic: better the garage than the house in cold weather.

Order Rhamphorhynchia
SORDES

In the Soviet Union Sordes is known also as "Hairy Devil" and "filthy feet"! It is, without doubt, a filthy, hairy devil. Perhaps because of this it has undoubted fascination and charm.

L ike nearly all pterosaurs, *Sordes* is covered with thick fur, even underneath the wing membrane. The long, prehensile tail is not attached to this membrane, which extends as far as the hind legs. Different species have slightly different coloured fur, but in the most common, *S. pilosus,* the fur is dark reddish-brown.

The nose is sharp and the mouth full of teeth, which are used with some restraint (but not much). The eyes are huge, dark and liquid; it is these that exert that fascination which is later regretted so half-heartedly. For though *Sordes* is a dirty little devil, it is a charming one too. If you find things difficult to forgive, obtain a little Hairy Devil: you will discover a host of acts that need to be forgiven, and a newly acquired ability to do so. Its mellowing influence under provoking circumstances – indeed, its very ability to provoke the type of circumstances that require the mellowed response –

have made it particularly popular in psychiatric hospitals in its native country.

They are omnivores: feeding them is no problem. More of a problem is their tendency to feed on the most unexpected, not to say unwanted, organic material, and their ingenuity in getting to it. They are messy feeders and totally uninterested in grooming themselves, so you will find it necessary to bath them from time to time. They enjoy this: use a soft scrubbing brush and powerful shampoo or detergent. Avoid the temptation to tickle your *Sordes.*

Give your *Sordes* a draught-proof corner, with plenty of branches, horizontal bars or (best) vertical blankets to hang from. Bother less about security than luxury – a sensible attitude in many aspects of life – for *Sordes* will remain where it is most comfortable.

Wear protective clothing when playing with your *Sordes,* and try not to let it in the house.

Order Rhamphorhynchia
ANUROGNATHUS

One of the best-looking of the pterosaurs, Anurognathus is ideal for the pond-owner who wants something more original than ornamental waterfowl.

A nurognathus is a very aquatic species whose yellow beak and matching hind flippers make it perhaps the most attractive of the pterosaurs. Its fur is a very dark, glossy brown, almost black.

Its food in the wild is fish, crayfish, frogs, small tortoises and so on, and you should try to reproduce this diet as exactly as you can in captivity. Lameness or partial paralysis when they occur are due to a de-

ficiency of Vitamin D or lime. Try massaging legs and wings with methylated spirit.

As regards accommodation, water is essential, circulating constantly to prevent its becoming foul. A medium-sized pond of a couple of acres, netted over at twenty feet or so, should make excellent quarters for a couple of pairs. Beautiful and rather characterless – a depressingly common combination – in both sexes. Keep them as ornaments, but do not expect a lot of fun.

Order Pterodactylia
PTERODACTYLUS ELEGANS

This charming and popular handkerchief-sized pterodactyl may be kept in the house. Easily house-trained and happy in the hurly-burly of family life, they are easily fed and bred.

An appealing and tiny pterodactyl, about six inches long, with small teeth in the front of the jaw only. The bull has a golden crown and a blue bib; the cow and calves are much more uniformly coloured, but there are usually some greenish streaks on breast and flanks and a buffish stripe over the eye. *P. elegans* is social to the point of gregariousness and should, if at all possible, be kept in small herds of twenty or so. Alternatively, single specimens, especially bulls, may be kept in the house, rather like a cat or bantam hen. Give them as large a cage as you can manage with plenty of perches and allow them the run of the house as often as possible. They are easily (but not quickly) house-trained, and are happiest in the confusion of family life; children are particularly valuable to absorb some of the animal high spirits usually shown by healthy and affectionate bulls.

They love to play hide and seek, preferring to hide rather than seek, and hugely enjoy the surprise aspect of this game. In fact, they frequently hide even when the game has not been suggested, and pop out at you, and especially your visitors, making a low cooing noise, which some wrongly construe as their way of saying "boo". In fact, they make this not unpleasant noise on other occasions – when you trip up, when you spill something, when your car won't start – and it is quite clear that what they are doing is laughing. They are not recommended for the aged, the nervous or the paranoid.

P. elegans is an insectivore: in summer it can catch its own food outside (though this may not be feasible in some areas). In other seasons, mealworms and gentles are a good basic diet, and you can experiment with other particulate food. Try small biscuits, vitamin capsules (especially D), liver shreds and soy bean mini cutlets.

Order Pterodactylia
CRIORHYNCHUS

A lovely pterosaur with a lovely nature, easily assimilated into the family scene. Easily fed, gentle and beautiful, it flourishes luxuriantly in the home and can be treated as one of the family.

This rare and unusual ornithocheirid is my own personal favourite among the pterosaurs. It is unusual in having a very short rounded head, which gives it a charm shared only by the horrid Hairy Devil, *Sordes* (page 21).

Criorhynchus is easily tamed and house-trained. All it needs is a parrot-style perch above a tray. It is gentle and will not harm babies. The reverse is not always true, and you must keep all babies away from any household containing *Criorhynchus*. It has only a few large teeth. What it eats in the wild is unknown, but in the home it will eat any meaty food. Some claim their *Criorhynchus* eats what and where they do.

Captive *Criorhynchus* will not breed, though they flourish. They will court, but that's as far as it goes, even under conditions of extreme privacy. This invariably leads to scarcity in captivity; indeed, this coyness may extend to their behaviour in the wild.

Order Pterodactylia

DSUNGARIPTERUS

*A highly recommended species. A calf hand-reared from the egg becomes very tame. It will live
happily in a garden that has a pond, and at night is happy to hang up on the gutter.*

I n *Dsungaripterus* the teeth have been lost from the front part of the jaws, which are used as fish-spears. As usual, the underside is white and the back grey.

It eats lots of fish. If feeding is a problem, become a fisherman or place a regular wholesale order with your fishmonger. Because of its large size and fishy diet, *Dsungaripterus* is best kept in a very large outdoor aviary enclosing a lake, but it is very accommodating about its accommodation. If a calf is raised from the egg, it will become extremely tame and loathe to leave what it considers its home. Although too big to allow inside any but the stateliest homes, it *will* happily live in a garden, as long as there is a largish pond in it. At night it likes to hang itself up by its toes on the roof or gutter, where it is troubled only by the fiercest weather. Although wide, *Dsungaripterus* is light and delicate and in windy weather may become entangled in branches, wires and so on. All the larger pterosaurs have trouble with wind and should be kept indoors when the Beaufort Scale exceeds 4. If you live in a chronically windy place, such as Tierra del Fuego, where there is very little chance of flight outside, a large aircraft hangar with a pond in it should be provided, with ledges for the pterosaur to depend on. Usually *Dsungaripterus* will manage to cope with bluster and carry on hanging regardless.

This is an intelligent animal which can be trained by rewarding it with fish. Since it is hanging on the roof of your house at night anyway, it is worth training it to spear intruders. Be sure to teach it to distinguish between bona fide visitors and the unwelcome. Tell your friends to whistle some well-known tune, like *Davy Crockett, My Way* or John Cage's *Apartment House 1776,* as they approach your house and reward *Dsungaripterus* when it does not attack people whistling the chosen tune. A useful side-effect is that insurance salesmen, children who have kicked balls into your garden and worthy people collecting for charity quickly learn not to bother you. You can try to protect such people by putting up a large notice: "Beware of the Dsungaripterus", but most of them won't know what it means, and those that do will almost certainly dismiss it as a joke.

Breeding is fairly regular, producing two elliptical eggs. Some individuals seem ignorant of proper incubation procedures. In these cases it is best to remove the eggs and incubate them yourself. Airing cupboards are often recommended, but results are patchy. Putting the eggs in bed with you at night and under an electric blanket (set to high) in the daytime is still the best bet, and has produced surprising results.

Riding *Ornithomimus* is not as easy as it looks. Don't try to trot before you can walk.

·DINOSAURS·
for
RIDING

Suborder Theropoda

ORNITHOMIMUS

An appealing first dinosaur for the child anxious for her first ride. Easy to break in and tractable. Undemanding to feed. Conveniently housed in your paddock.

If you want to keep something more exciting than the more usual coelurosaur, *Ornithomimus* is an ideal beginner's choice. It has a tiny head, a bird-like beak, seldom any teeth, long, thin, avian legs, and a long tail stiffened as a counterbalance to the long neck. The larger species, sixteen feet long, are admittedly a little awkward and yet, in spite of their bulk, they are very amenable to captivity. They have no claws that catch; they don't bite; they rely on avoiding their enemies and, to this end, their legs, like Helena's, are longer to run away. For a dinosaur, *Ornithomimus* has a larger than average brain. A tamed individual is gentle and easily trained, and can be ridden with a saddle. A fractious one can annihilate with a kick, so a gentle specimen is recommended. The smaller species, six to eight feet in length, can be kept in a paddock and broken in for children; the larger ones are very exciting to ride.

Learning to ride *Ornithomimus* is more like learning to ride a bicycle than a horse: your principal concern at first is to gain faith in your combined ability to stand up. Once this is achieved, you find that the creature's walk is secure and sedate; unfortunately this gives many novice riders an unwarranted sense of confidence which prompts them to try trotting, for the trot is best described as a rhythmic earthquake: the animal lurches from side to side as the weight is jerkily transferred from one foot to the other and the unpracticed rider is shaken almost senseless as he struggles desperately to slow the creature back down to a walk.

It is best to leave trotting to those who have made a hobby, and sometimes a profession, out of *Ornithomimus* dressage. The beginner should walk the animal on roads and move it swiftly to a canter and then a gallop when he reaches grass. The cantering *Ornithomimus* is another curious spectacle. The animal keeps its legs straight and "skips", and the rider finds that his body above the waist takes on a rhythmical twisting motion – one shoulder forward then the other – rather like someone drying his back in slow motion. This is not as painful as trotting, but it is nonetheless inelegant. Move up to a gallop as soon as you can, for a galloping *Ornithomimus* simply runs with its head stretched forward; the upper part of its body becomes stable and the rider at last feels comfortable and able to acknowledge the cheers of his friends.

Ornithomimus is one of the easiest dinosaurs to feed as it will eat all brands of dog- and cat-food as well as most scraps from the table. Like the ostrich, it is a gastronomic polymath. Feed it a small mammal, such as a mouse, vole or stoat, as an occasional treat.

This is the only dinosaur species I can think of in which copulation occurs *after* egg-laying and *before* hatching. *Ornithomimus* can be bred without any great difficulty. The chicks, when hatched, are protected by the female. At seven weeks or so, the mother relaxes and the young can be removed from her care. Such a home-hatched chick is ideal for training.

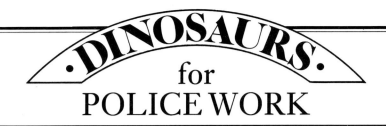

·DINOSAURS· for POLICE WORK

Order Pseudosuchia
SCLEROMOCHLUS

*A charming little pseudosuchian, easily fed. Although difficult to train, you
can collar it and exercise it on a chain. Useful as a guard in your yard.*

This lightly built little dinosaur is about three feet long, and half of this is tail. It is not unlike a wallaby in shape, with large hind legs and small front legs, although the forearms are long. Like a wallaby it moves by hopping along; unlike a wallaby it walks on its hind legs without the help of a tail or front legs. This is a loyal and reasonably intelligent creature, which could be of great use to security organisations.

Although carnivorous, *Scleromochlus* is suitable for the beginner. It will eat most recognized dog-foods, meaty scraps of various sorts, and eggs. You can persuade tame specimens to wear a collar and exercise them outside, in street or park, in the same way that you would exercise a wallaby. In spite of their jumping capacity they are good climbers: a *Scleromochlus* should be provided with a tree or some large shrubs to scramble about in. Their ability to jump and climb makes them difficult pets to contain within an appointed area, and they can only be allowed in the house under supervision. However, if you keep *Scleromochlus* on a running lead in your yard, it will bark – or rather squeal – at intruders and jump on them if they come near enough.

Suborder Theropoda
VELOCIRAPTOR

*A splendid, loyal, fierce friend. For the country sportsman who wants real
sport, or for the police force that needs to get its man.*

This small, agile carnivore has slender legs and long, clutching hands, and is nine feet long. It is very much a flesh-eater, needing meat in large quantities: some specimens can be weaned on to corned beef but this is not really economical. It is intelligent and will respond to rigorous training.

Velociraptor is, at its best, a splendid, loyal creature. It can be fierce, it is true, and some individuals seem untameable. They can inflict severe wounds, and strange children should not, as a general rule, be encouraged to stroke or pet them. But the right animal in the right hands is a marvellous combination. Tame dinosaurs may be taken for runs in the country, where they will soon catch their own prey. They should, therefore, be kept clear of sheep, goats, calves, pigs and small people. Give them short, sharp names, like Butch, Max or Jane.

Suborder Theropoda
COELOPHYSIS

Fast, agile and inquisitive, an entertaining and easily fed coelurosaur. A perfect dinosaur for catching people, but easily tamed and suitable for a young childless couple.

This is a typical coelurosaur and is very slender. Its *métier* is agility. Its long, thin neck ends in a small head with jaws full of tiny saw-edged teeth. It has a long, thin tail to balance its long, thin neck, and long, thin, back legs which it runs on. On its forelegs it has hands with three long, thin fingers. The biggest *Coelophysis* is about ten feet long from tip of nose to tip of tail, but it weighs less than fifty pounds.

Coelophysis is carnivorous, but will happily settle for all sorts of vaguely meaty food. It seems to eat almost anything given to it as long as it is not too overtly vegetable: eggs, fish, cat-food, dog-food, parrot-food, muesli, granola, corned beef and so on. It rejects curry. Most dinosaurs, and *Coelophysis* is no exception, like such green leaves as lettuce, chickweed, dandelion and viper's bugloss from time to time and especially during the breeding season. It thrives on meat and two vegetables.

Coelophysis is an entertaining dinosaur, and because it is so fast and agile you will need to provide plenty of space and good fencing, preferably inturned at the top to prevent the animal climbing out. *Coelophysis* is very inquisitive and its long, grasping hands can be used to snatch, for instance, small lap-dogs which are then hurried away to be consumed at leisure. It can be a bit of a nuisance in this way, but with proper precautions it will become a merry pet, as long as you don't want to keep any other small animals or children.

Coelophysis won't attack anything larger than a medium-sized dog or a three-year-old child, unless trained to, and it is intelligent. It can therefore be taught to perform useful tasks in any situation where there are no small, living creatures. For example, tennis players find that *Coelophysis* make excellent ballboys; and they can be trained – by those prepared to persevere – to play triads on the piano with their three fingers. Some jazz pianists find it convenient to have *Coelophysis* playing rhythmical right-hand parts so that they can concentrate on developing chord sequences in the left hand.

Coelophysis' greatest potential, however, is as an aid to the police and intelligence services, for they can run faster than any human and can be trained to obey commands. A top *Coelophysis* working with a skilled handler will apprehend, but not kill, even in the most extreme circumstances. It revels in its speed and its ability to dodge machine-gun fire, bazookas, Exocet missiles and the like.

Coelophysis will breed readily, in normal coelurosaur fashion, but is prone to egg binding.

Suborder Theropoda
ORNITHOLESTES

Perhaps less suitable than Coelophysis for domestic use but eminently suitable for the apprehension of suspected malefactors. Would suit rural police force.

Reminiscent of *Coelophysis, Ornitholestes* is, at six feet long, a slightly more formidable carnivore. It, too, has long, thin legs, and arms with grasping fingers, balanced by a very long, stiff tail. In spite of its height it is unexpectedly light, as its bones are filled with air.

Ornitholestes is an active hunter in the wild, and catches small reptiles and mammals, or the young of other dinosaurs. It is a scavenger too, occupying to some extent the ecological niche filled in modern Africa by hyaenas and jackals. Feeding is, therefore, no great problem: plenty of offal twice a week keeps it healthy and happy.

It is fairly tractable if brought up from the egg; indeed, many specimens obtained as adults adapt easily to the conditions of captivity, particularly (it must be said) males. The female is more difficult in this respect, although once she *has* adapted herself she makes a more satisfactory captive than the male.

It can be trained for the same tasks as *Coelophysis,* although more care must be taken to prevent it maiming its captives. The same sorts of conditions should be provided as for *Coelophysis.* It is not so easy to catch, although the reverse is not true. Even less safe with small children than *Coelophysis.* It is sometimes, and more correctly, known as *Coelurus.*

Suborder Theropoda
STENONYCHOSAURUS

Perhaps the most rewarding of the dromaeosaurs, small, agile, bipedal and immensely intelligent. As a guard or friend it can scarcely be bettered, being loyal and easily trained.

Although *Stenonychosaurus* is bigger than many birds, it has a very bird-like appearance. It has an intelligent look about it, a genuine desire to please and the ability to perform really useful tasks. It is small and agile, with slender legs and long, clutching hands; it is wholly bipedal and therefore chic.

Chained in your yard, it will alert you to intruders; but best of all it can be taught at the ring of a bell to put out plates and cups, squeeze oranges, grind coffee, remove the lids from yogurt cartons and make toast. Keep it on a long leash in your kitchen at night, therefore, and give it a hug and let it sit with you at table whenever it achieves this satisfactorily.

Like the other dromaeosaurs, *Stenonychosaurus* is carnivorous and needs plenty of good, red meat. If you obtain one young, either a female or a male will prove responsive, though it may display its gentle side only to its owner. Most specimens do not quite reach six feet in length, and half of this is tail: so it is manageable, though looking after it can be a bit of a Sisyphean labour. You should *always* keep it on a lead when it is not in its stout cage: its long hands are quite capable of clutching dogs and other passing animals, which may then be summarily dispatched. Even on a lead, *Stenonychosaurus* must be kept clear of baby carriages outside shops. Nevertheless, sensibly directed its great intelligence makes it an excellent companion.

Suborder Theropoda
DEINONYCHUS

For the careful and socially responsible owner, an entire flock is most fulfilling. For a government seeking an unconventional weapon, this species could be the answer. See picture on page 4.

A typical deinonychosaur, *Deinonychus* is about three feet high. It is a carnivore, with powerful teeth and jaws; and its arms are long and gangling, with three long-clawed fingers on each hand. The hind legs are particularly remarkable: two of the claws are walked upon; a third one is held up off the ground and forward. This third claw is five inches long, razor sharp and sickle-shaped. It can be swung through 180 degrees to project downward and backward and is used to disembowel prey which is held by the forearms at the appropriate distance (arm's length). The long tail is rigid and horizontal and acts as a balancing rod.

Deinonychus is exclusively carnivorous and requires its food in great, bleeding chunks: a standing order with your butcher is needed. Ideally it should be given young piglets or lambs. Throw them into the enclosure entire, and avert your eyes. Pigeons and guinea pigs are also much appreciated. It will not eat mice or other small mammals, nor can it be trained to take dog-foods (although dogs are another matter). Add to this the fact that *Deinonychus* will not thrive by itself, and it becomes clear that this dinosaur cannot be kept on the cheap.

There is one other major problem – the third claw. This is designed for eviscerating and human victims

are not uncommon: one angry swipe is enough, and no amount of pretence (and they are heart-rendingly penitent, believe me) can bring the victim back to life. *A private owner must trim the third claw.* (A small operation, similar to pinioning in wildfowl, can now be carried out, at some expense, whereby the last finger-joint is removed. The animal is unimpaired in its movement and lethal no longer.) *Deinonychus* rarely, if ever, bites in anger.

There is no doubt that it flourishes only if kept in groups of at least five.

Deinonychus is an extremely intelligent dinosaur; as it was discovered only in 1969 there has been very little opportunity to see to what extent it can be useful to its owner. However, a handful of advanced dinosaur-keepers who have been through the other intelligent species – *Gallimimus, Dsungaripterus, Dromaeosaurus, Stenonychosaurus et al.* – have managed to tame *Deinonychus* and thereafter to train it and test its intelligence. There are several *Deinonychus* who can play Happy Families – and are indeed brought together by their owners to play in tournaments against each other. These are colourful occasions, to which the public is admitted. The dinosaurs play in groups of four, sitting at small tables as in kindergarten. Attempts to teach them Monopoly are progressing only slowly.

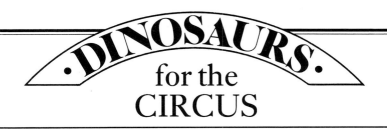

·DINOSAURS·
for the
CIRCUS

Suborder Theropoda
GALLIMIMUS

As well as its great appeal to circus proprietors, Gallimimus is an ideal dromaeosaur for beginners: small ones can be house-trained and are good with children. Usually easily fed.

This dromaeosaur, as its name suggests, is chicken-like in appearance, with a long neck, and is about 13 feet long. Some chicken! Some neck! Unlike a chicken, *Gallimimus* must have a mainly meaty diet. It despises biscuits.

Gallimimus is ideal for the novice dromaeosaur-keeper: it can even be house-trained, in all senses of the word, and is gentle enough not to worry children, though babies are a temptation. Its greatest qualities are its keenness to please and its boundless sense of fun. It can be trained to perform acts of daring, such as jumping through hoops of fire and walking the tightrope, as well as acts of straight-faced stoicism, such as standing still while custard pies are pushed into its face. They are difficult to breed, but success has been reported in Oldham, Lancashire and in Norfolk, Virginia. If you want to have a go, try raising the temperature to, say, the high eighties Fahrenheit and sprinkling both sexes (at the same time) with warm water. A plastic cage within a well-heated bathroom makes an ideal love-nest. Always keep *Galliminus* warm and provide plenty of toys and playmates.

Suborder Theropoda
DROMAEOSAURUS

An interesting and uncompromising dinosaur, probably unsuitable for the domestic owner but an exciting challenge for the Big Top.

My notes for this dinosaur, after whom the dromaeosaurs are named, read: carnivore, big brain, trenchant teeth, skilful killer, strongly recurved hind claw for lacerating, agile, dexterous, huge eyes, grasping hands, overly libidinous. A frightening list of attributes, coupled with its large size (much bigger than *Deinonychus*). In my opinion the private collector should leave this creature to the professionals: if you must try your hand with it, wear a suit of armour. (Plate armour must be used, for chain mail bruises the wearer and damages the dinosaur's toes. Japanese and other Eastern armour is insufficient.)

Lion tamers, who have grown bored with their work, will want to try their hands at *Dromaeosaurus*. It is intelligent but fierce, entertaining but dangerous. I recommend 'pinioning' it before public display (see *Deinonychus*, page 29). The person who can put his head into the jaws of *Dromaeosaurus*, while wearing a sequinned leotard, will shoot to stardom.

·DINOSAURS·
for
EGGS

Suborder Ornithopoda
PSITTACOSAURUS

Here is a perfectly decent dinosaur for the family, and full of eggs. It can bite, so don't play silly games with it.

A parrot-faced dinosaur up to eight feet long. It has big hands for grasping plants and a big beak for chewing them. It is both quadrupedal and bipedal. It eats tough plants such as shrubs and trees, which it can chop up with its beak. These should be provided fresh. Keep, say, half a dozen in a small field and fence it well.

For breeding or egg-laying, give it the same conditions as *Protoceratops* (page 33). Remove the eggs the same day that they are laid in the nest, which *Psittacosaurus* builds itself. It will then lay more for you. Even so there is a limit to the number it will lay. Deep freezing them after hard-boiling may be the way to ensure a regular supply. You can also freeze Dinosaur-egg Florentine.

Most dinosaur eggs, *Psittacosaurus* included, taste somewhat like ostrich eggs and are therefore becoming a fashionable delicacy, fetching high prices. The vogue is to serve them hard-boiled with a dinosaur-egg mayonnaise: one egg provides at least four portions. For advice on cracking them, see *Anatosaurus,* page 34. Dinosaur egg-boxes will soon be available.

Suborder Ornithopoda
HYPSILOPHODON

A very manageable source of winter eggs. Tame, friendly and adaptable. Failures with this timid creature occur only if you expect it to climb trees. Give it space.

A little charmer about four feet long and two feet high, commonest in the Isle of Wight, England. It has rows of bony plates in the skin of its back. It is bipedal and has a long, very stiff tail which it uses to balance itself, especially when running, which it does very quickly and very often. It has a row of small teeth on its upper jaw at the front of its mouth, and eats mainly fruit and leaves. It does not eat grass. Make fresh food available to it at all times, soft rather than hard.

Hypsilophodon needs space. It is an exceptionally agile and speedy sprinter, and if confined it becomes constipated, mopes and dies. Do not crowd its enclosure with trees: it doesn't climb; indeed, it cannot.

If you obtain it as a chick, *Hypsilophodon* becomes markedly tame and friendly, but it is naturally timid and prone to panic. Keep it outdoors in summer and in a big, heated enclosure in winter. Eggs are sure to come. It is suitable for children and will enjoy winning races with them, but is impossible to housetrain.

Suborder Ceratopsia
PROTOCERATOPS

An easily-fed dinosaur that lays large numbers of eggs: conveniently paddocked in scrub in summer and housed indoors in winter. Quite easily bred.

A t only six feet long, *Protoceratops* is a relatively small dinosaur, and (together with *Leptoceratops,* page 13) by far the easiest of the frilled ones. It has no horns, only a small frill, and is a quadruped.

Protoceratops is totally herbivorous and easily fed. It likes tough stuff such as entire shrubs. In temperate climates you can enclose some of them in an acre or two of scrubland where they will be happy tucking into bramble, hawthorn, elder, sloe, and so on.

Bring them indoors in winter. The floor should be well-drained. If it is concrete it must have a good, thick covering of sand, sawdust, or peat. For maximum egg-production, strip lighting is best, and fluorescent cheapest to run. Provide heat spots for sunbathing by installing spot lights every few feet.

As long as both sexes are present, they will lay large numbers of large eggs in large nests which they scrape in the ground.

Protoceratops relies on the heat of the sun to incubate the eggs. If you want them to hatch in cool areas, you must carefully unearth the eggs and incubate them artificially. Most airing cupboards are far too small; you will need a larger, warm, moist chamber. A sauna is ideal.

Undesirable hard-shelled eggs can be detected by their unexpected heaviness, together with a much more opaque appearance than usual. The hard shell causes late hatching as well as problems for anyone eating them. Moisten the eggs daily (twice daily when humidity is low) in warm water.

Rearing the chicks is best left to the parents if at all possible. Watch carefully: if either parent shows hostility you may have to do the rearing yourself. I can offer little guidance: expect problems and counter them with common sense.

If you want to use the eggs as food, make sure that you gather them soon after laying, and eat them soon after gathering. They don't like having their eggs taken away and in the wild will fight – on occasion to the death – with *Velociraptors* who try to raid their nests. They may get used to losing them in time, but at first it is advisable either to take the eggs under cover of darkness – when there is danger of your treading on a slumbering *Protoceratops* – or, better, to create some sort of diversion. This shouldn't be anything which will make them panic, as fireworks surely will, rather some spectacle without too great a surprise element, such as a juggling *Gallimimus* or even someone doing an impression of Groucho Marx. They will stand still and gape at anything of this nature, leaving you quite safe to take their eggs.

Suborder Ornithopoda
ANATOSAURUS

Arguably the best hadrosaur for the farmer familiar with sandy soil; big, gentle and easily bred, they can also be decorative in safari-parks, and are wonderful layers.

A fine group of dinosaurs classified under the ornithopods are the hadrosaurs or Duck-Billed Dinosaurs. There are more than thirty species of hadrosaurs and with them we move closer to the layman's conventional, or B-movie style, dinosaur (although there is a long way to go yet), for these are on average 30 feet long, 13 feet high, and weigh about three tons. However, there is no cause for alarm. Although they cannot be brought into the average home, they are gentle creatures, pre-eminently suitable for farming, who will harm no one unless provoked. Indeed the problem with them is that they can become quite affectionate, and they show their affection by hugging its object with their short, strong forelegs. There are no reports of any fatalities as a result of this, but several people have survived only after mouth-to-mouth resuscitation, and in one at least of these cases this was performed, haphazardly but effectively, by the very hadrosaur who had administered the knock-out squeeze. So, play hard to get, always be ready to run, and don't let them get too involved with children or the elderly.

Perhaps the hadrosaur's least characteristic feature is the one that gives it its familiar English name of Duck-Billed Dinosaur. It does have a rounded upper jaw with a flat tip bearing a horny beak which it uses to crop foliage, but in living hadrosaurs this structure is often hidden by the muscles of the face and jaws and it does not then look in the least duck-billed. I am tempted to think that the man who gave them their popular name had never seen them in the wild. There is usually a crest down the centre of the back and the stiff tail. The neck is mobile and the skin is covered with a mosaic of small scales or nodules, and is often strikingly patterned. Some species are flat-headed, some have solid crests and some have hollow crests. They are not very bright, with a brain weighing about 1/20,000 of their body weight.

If you are the owner of a few hundred acres of pine forest the feeding can be cheap, although you will need a heated shed in winter. They breed readily in captivity, laying eggs in large communal nests. The meat is good, very much like frog without those irritating little bones. Instead of building a shed specially, you may find it simpler to convert an existing structure such as a coach-house, mews, ballroom, conservatory, redundant church or moat.

Hadrosaurs are best kept in mixed-sex groups of up to half a dozen, where their benevolently episcopal appearance, their gentle natures and their wholesome lack of initiative will be continually rewarding.

Anatosaurus is a delightful hadrosaur and is especially recommended. It has no crest and can be described as a typical flat-headed duckbill. The fingers of its hands are webbed and it likes the opportunity for a swim. When water in large quantities is not available you must provide a bath every second or third day: *fresh* bath water and in the mornings only, so that the animals do not roost while still damp. *Anatosaurus* is a catholic browser and will eat seeds, fruit and twigs.

Anatosaurus eggs are about nine inches long and, even for dinosaur eggs, are notoriously hard to crack. If an egg is for frying, scrambling or an omelette, use an electric drill with a half-inch masonry bit and help the contents out with a narrow fork. As yet there are few people who want to, or can, eat an entire *Anatosaurus* egg at one sitting. However, served soft-boiled (allow 26 minutes furious boiling) with a loaf of French bread to dip in, they make a convenient meal for those who only have time to eat once a day. To open any boiled *Hadrosaur* egg, engrave a circle with a diamond-tipped rotary glass cutter, strike the cut area with a hammer, and lift away with a rubber suction pad (a toy arrow is ideal). A patent dinosaur egg-opener will shortly be available in hardware stores and works rather like a wall-mounted can-opener. A table version, incorporating a dinosaur egg-cup and reservoirs for salt and pepper, will soon be tested on a random sample of the general public.

Suborder Ornithopoda
PARASAUROLOPHUS

Ideal for farmers living on otherwise uninhabited islands. Easily fed and cared for,
Parasaurolophus is a wonderful source of eggs, meat, and company for the hard of hearing.

This majestic dinosaur bears a hollow crest more than six feet long. With an overall length of more than thirty-two feet, and its immense fertility, it is potentially the most valuable hadrosaur, for both meat and eggs. But it does have a major drawback: it is very noisy. The hollow crest contains the air passage from lungs to mouth and acts as a resonator. The booming bellows of this extrovert dinosaur make farming it possible only in remote areas, far from human habitation.

And, like so many of the dinosaurs, *Parasaurolophus* has a sense of humour and a love of surprise. If you are of a gentle, contemplative nature and like from time to time to stand quietly musing on a flower or to sit in some private nook reading a favourite poem, *Parasaurolophus* is probably not for you. He will seek you out, creep stealthily up behind you, put his lips to your ear, hold his breath for an instant and then let out a primeval noise, similar to the foghorn of an ocean liner.

Despite this a cult of *Parasaurolophus* fanciers has grown up, and the Friends of Parasaurolophus Society (FOPS) now has branches in several countries. FOPS tell me that they will soon be launching a major programme of *Parasaurolophus* shows, which will be held regularly in remote places. Enthusiasts and their dinosaurs will travel the long distances involved in specially soundproofed pantechnicons. Males will be judged on the size and shape of their crests and females on the regularity and colouring of their skin markings. Account will be taken in both sexes of the clarity of the eyes, which are some four inches across, and eggs will be judged for size and colouring. These will obviously be very colourful events and an excellent pastime for people with low conversational skills; all participants will wear either ear plugs or Walkman radios and communicate in sign language. The judges will hold up cards as at ice-skating competitions and the scores, for no reason that I can understand, will range between 6.1 and 7.

DINOSAURS
for
PELAGE AND PLUMAGE

Order Pseudosuchia
LONGISQUAMA

A friendly little fellow, brightly coloured and covered with feathery frills. Not difficult to feed and thrives in company. The feathers may be collected annually, during the moult.

The "feathers" of *Longisquama* are used mainly for decoration. This is a small pseudosuchian – about three feet long – with a curious appearance, owing partially to its being covered with scales, some of which – the ones along the hind edge of the front legs – have the appearance of feathers, projecting as they do like little frills. But the most striking feature of *Longisquama* is the row of long scales above its backbone from neck to pelvis. These are brightly coloured (the colours varying in different species) and can be raised or lowered.

It eats fruit, dragonflies and some bumble bees: a bizarre diet. It will accept various commercial brands of monkey food; also eggs and *some* kitchen scraps. Not as difficult as it might seem.

Longisquama is yet another charmer; it is friendly and generally unaggressive, and enjoys playing with children and being taken for walks. However, it is not very intelligent and the only trick it can be taught – by rewarding it with dragonflies, bumble bees or canned peaches – is to raise its scaly crest on command. The novelty of a single *Longisquama* doing this wears off rather quickly, and the neighbours will become bored. However, if you can train a troupe of, say, six *Longisquamas* to raise and lower their crests in unison and to music, you will find yourself greatly in demand and may even be able to turn professional. Start them off on the slowest music you can find: any Leonard Cohen number or any Gregorian chant will do. Move on to waltzes and ballads, such as *The Blue Danube* or *The Teddy Bears' Picnic,* and when the muscles really develop try *The Flight of the Bumble Bee* or *Rock Around the Clock.*

Although *Longisquama* is covered with insulating scales it is only little and should be given a warmed enclosure in winter. Give it plenty of shrubs or branches in its securely roofed pen, and lots of sunshine; in winter supplement this with ultra-violet lamps.

It is happiest kept with others in groups of half a dozen or so. Breeding is simple: pairing takes place after a spectacular crest-waving courtship. From seven to nine eggs are laid in the sand. These should be artificially heated by ultra-violet lamps if they are to hatch in temperate countries.

Moulting occurs annually at the end of summer and you should gather the scaly "feathers" then. They are strikingly unusual when worn in hats, and have become especially popular in the alpine districts of Germany and Switzerland. The longer feathers are much prized by woodwind players of all nationalities for clearing their instruments and annoying the violas.

Longisquama is prone to depluming scabies, which is caused by mites irritating the skin so that the animal tears its "feathers" out. Dip the infected dinosaur in a solution of 2 oz soft soap and 2 oz flowers of sulphate in 1 gal of water at 100°F, then let it dry in a *warm* room. Spray the living quarters (*Longisquama's*) with creosote and air them.

Suborder Ankylosauria
THE ANKYLOSAURS

*Slow, squat and dangerous, the Ankylosaurs nonetheless have their
admirers. The hides are remarkable and much prized.*

For those who enthuse over tanks – and there are many such people – there is nothing to beat an ankylosaur: heavy, well-armoured, slow, expensive to run and occasionally deadly. Quite what the enthusiasts find attractive in these almost reptilian creatures is a mystery to me, but they help to prove that there is a dinosaur to suit every taste. By dinosaur standards they are not all that difficult to keep. The golden rule is: keep clear of the tail, especially if you have *Euoplocephalus* or *Scolosaurus* (see page 41).

Feeding arrangements are the same for all of them. As a general rule, the slower and more heavily armoured they are, the less fussy they are with their food. Horsetails of the vegetable sort are a good basic, but you should supplement these with soft vegetables and soft fruit. Try commercial cakes, deciduous leaves, soft bark, *Brassica,* peaches, pomegranates, pineapples or passion-fruit. No success in breeding yet; if you wish to encourage it, you may find it worthwhile to install a sprinkler system: many dinosaurs are brought into the mood by rain.

For the summer months they will do best outside. A pit should be excavated to a depth of a few feet, then enclosed with a brick wall high enough to keep the animals in: ten feet should suffice. You should drive

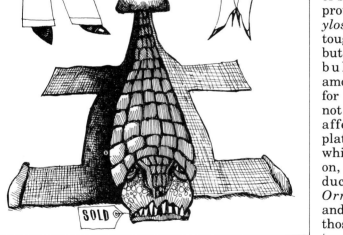

SOLD

sheets of steel in to a depth of several feet, right around the perimeter, to prevent escape by burrowing. Line the enclosure with at least two feet of concrete: the club-tailed ankylosaurs can demolish most walls in a few seconds. Inside the enclosure supply plenty of loose, friable soil and some largish boulders to provide adequate hiding places for nervous individuals. There must be an abundant supply of water, for drinking and cooling. A heated indoor pit of similar design should be provided for winter. *Ankylosaur* hide is extremely tough and difficult to bend, but it is proof against some bullets; so the trend amongst film and pop stars for covering cars with it is not just a publicity-seeking affectation. The spikes, plates, warts and nodules, which the superstars leave on, can be filed off to produce durable saddles for *Ornithomimus* or horses and excellent knee pads for those who clean floors in the traditional way. Don't bother with the meat; no amount of cooking can make it remotely chewable, although zoos can, of course, feed it raw to *Tyrannosaurus.*

The six most popular species are discussed overleaf. All but *Acanthopholis,* for whom there is little enthusiasm, are shown in competitions where they are judged on the quality of their armour. *Ankylosaur* shows are usually held in disused reservoirs.

Suborder Ankylosauria
ACANTHOPHOLIS

A perfectly decent, small, highly armoured ankylosaur, very much underestimated by amateur and connoisseur alike. Easily fed and, given the means, easily housed.

*A*canthopholis is about thirteen feet long and its back is covered with thick bony plates, with short spikes about the shoulders. It is definitely a quadruped and has a slightly arched back.

Like all ankylosaurs, it eats soft vegetable matter. Cryptogamous plants, such as horsetails, are prefer-red, but the usual commercial winter feeds should suffice. Be alert for vitamin deficiency.

Acanthopholis is the least military of the ankylosaurs and, for that reason perhaps, the least popular: too reptilian for most dinosaur-lovers, too mainstream for the tank brigade. Take it for what it is, a slightly bendy, reasonably pleasant creature.

Suborder Ankylosauria
POLACANTHUS

A somewhat ponderous dinosaur, covered with spikes, warts and plates. With its own spacious, centrally-heated pit it offers unexpected rewards to the discerning owner.

*W*ith *Polacanthus* we get a taste of the *grotesquerie* so beloved by the ankylosaur-fancier, but the underlying body, though thickset, is still relatively flexible. At fifteen feet long *Polacanthus* is more of a heavily armoured car than a tank. On its neck, back and shoulders are seven pairs of massive spikes, over its hind legs is a heavy bony plate, and its tail is decorated with a double row of vertical bony slabs. Of all the ankylosaur hides, *Polacanthus* – dividing as it does into three sections – probably makes the most suitable, and indeed eyecatching, protection for limousines: spikes at the front, bony plate on the roof and vertical slabs at the rear. It cannot stand grapes.

Suborder Ankylosauria
NODOSAURUS

The fussiest, but least dangerous ankylosaur. Although children should be kept away, it will quickly get to know its owner and has an unexpectedly charming nature.

*N*odosaurus is bigger and stockier than either of the foregoing: the armour consists of bony plates and warts rather than spikes.

As far as feeding is concerned, it is the hardest ankylosaur to please. The traditional British method of boiling vegetables will convert most plant material to the soft consistency appropriate.

This is the most manageable ankylosaur. Once it is familiar with someone, it will allow that person to clean its cage, and even the floor between its feet, without protest. Some owners claim that their *Nodosaurus* smiles at them from time to time. I suspect another explanation for this eerie grin: as with human babies.

Suborder Ankylosauria
PALAEOSCINCUS

This disagreeable animal can be kept like any other ankylosaur and might just appeal to a
wholesale fruiterer. It is, however, very untrustworthy and a dinosaur to avoid.

Many dinosaur-lovers will be surprised to find the dreaded *Palaeoscincus* included in this book. They rightly regard it as beyond the pale and its adherents as a lunatic fringe who give dinosaur-keeping a bad name. I include it for two reasons: first, I feel a duty to warn the unsuspecting public; secondly, like anything thoroughly tasteless, *Palaeoscincus* must enjoy a brief period of enormous popularity – and its time, unfortunately, is now. Hula-hoops, yoyos, frisbees, free love – and, for 1984, *Palaeoscincus*.

Superficially the creature is another squat tank. Its back and tail are covered with a carapace of horny plates, and a fringe of large bony spikes projects from its sides, close to and parallel with the ground, surrounding the animal from its neck to the end of its tail, which has a bony knob on its tip. The problems, however, stem from its mental attitude. It is aggressive, foul-tempered, unpredictable, hostile to all other living species, uninterested in personal freshness, impossible to please and sadistic. Unlike the numerous humans who exhibit these qualities, *Palaeoscincus* has not one redeeming feature. If you must have one – and do consider *Nodosaurus*, *Polacanthus* or even *Scolosaurus* first – you should take special precautions at all times and especially when providing food, to avoid death or injury. Wear plate armour as with *Dromaeosaurus* (page 31). *Palaeoscincus* has a habit of running sideways (not backwards) at a suspected enemy and impaling him on its spikes. If the intended victim dodges the first lateral onslaught the spiky tail is brought into play. Legs have been lost in this way. Never go within ten feet of *Palaeoscincus*, always be ready to run (it is slow moving), and above all make not even the tiniest attempt at friendship: *Palaeoscincus* delights in impaling the soft-hearted.

The usual ankylosaur feeding remarks pertain here, but *Palaeoscincus* is particularly fond of fruit. Berries are all useful when in season, but for the rest of the year you will have to rely on commercial fruits. Apples, pears, grapes and bananas will be usual standbys. Dried currants and raisins that have been soaked in warm water and then drained of surplus moisture are also good. Chopped dates and figs are useful, but sticky. Boiled rice or corn is welcomed.

Palaeoscincus, like other dinosaurs, may suffer from *Locomotor Ataxia*: the animal performs uncontrolled movements and presents a drunken appearance. Ataxia in the largest dinosaurs is the disease most likely to lead to destruction of property. As it is hereditary and incurable, you have an excuse for euthanasia.

Suborder Ankylosauria
SCOLOSAURUS

In Scolosaurus we have a dinosaur for the specialist. It is sullen, cantankerous and prone to constipation. Nevertheless, it is popular among ankylosaurophiles.

Scolosaurus consists of three and a half tons of bad tempered, motionless armour. It has plates and spikes on its back, and in appearance it is squat. For a tail it has a spined club, with which it is likely to flail out at the least provocation or none. Unlike *Palaeoscincus,* however, it can be lulled into a sleepy form of good humour. It will be transfixed by a metronome, a pendulum, a tennis match, or any form of kinetic sculpture. In this state it can be groomed for competition, driven about in trucks and even prodded by judges, without retaliating. Wear armour if you have to go close to it.

If you deviate from the menu I suggest on page 37, constipation may result. This is usually cured by giving extra greens and fruit. If it is stubborn, try that grand and traditional remedy, cod liver oil, either mixed with food or squirted straight into the mouth with, say, a fire extinguisher.

Suborder Ankylosauria
EUOPLOCEPHALUS

If you are really careful with its diet and can provide plenty of exercise, this formidable ankylosaur can be easily assimilated into the tolerant family circle.

About sixteen feet long, five tons in weight, with a tortoise-like carapace of bony plates over its back, this dinosaur has a bony lump on the end of its tail, which it uses like a shillelagh in defence. This is the most endearing of the ankylosaurs, a relatively sensitive creature which displays compassion and mercy: it will not attack an animal smaller than itself, unless very sorely provoked. Moreover, it will respond to friendly gestures, such as specially prepared food, a pat on the head or a walk outside its usual demesne. Keep it on a lead for such walks, and for safety's sake strap its tail to its back with a chain fastened around its middle. It will readily allow you to do this once it knows that this is a prelude to a walk. A well-tamed *Euoplocephalus* will allow children to ride on its back. This is perfectly safe, since the creature lumbers slowly along like an outsize tortoise.

The usual ankylosaur remarks apply to its diet, but *Euoplocephalus* does like its food soft. Overboil if necessary. If its diet is not to its liking, *Euoplocephalus* suffers from indigestion. Clues to this are dyspepsia and difficulty in passing droppings. This is often caused by too much or too little grit. Find out which and provide less or more. Remember that wood charcoal is necessary for all dinosaurs in captivity to absorb gases in the intestine and ward off flatulence, often a very considerable nuisance to the owners of the larger species.

I speak for myself when I say that I do not much care for ankylosaurs. I do not like tanks and I do not much like reptiles: ankylosaurs are very much one or the other or both. That said, I will confess to a soft spot for *Euoplocephalus* which almost avoids both traps: slightly too high in the legs for a successful tank, and not really reptilian in the sense that *Acanthopholis* is.

Suborder Ornithopoda
IGUANODON

*Docile to the point of soppiness, tractable, herdable and full of meat. Ideal for the farmer
with plenty of trees and shrubs. For obvious reasons it is unsuitable as a pet.*

I guanodon is a big dinosaur, thirty-five feet long and sixteen feet high, and it is mainly bipedal. It has a long tongue and a horny beak, four fingers and a thumb with a powerful spine; there are three hooved toes on each hind foot. Farmers whose only experience is with cattle should not be dismayed by the size of *Iguanodon*, for the creature is not only docile but amiable. Indeed, because of its size and tractability and the tastiness of its meat – somewhere between pork and lobster – *Iguanodon* is an ideal dinosaur for meat farming. The animals herd naturally and will eat almost all greenery with the exception of grass, using their many rows of leaf-shaped teeth. The males can be alarming when roused. However, they are only roused by thoughtless aggravation or if they are startled by something out of the ordinary – don't let a performing *Gallimimus* or anyone who dresses loudly into their pasture.

Like cattle they should be enclosed to prevent them straying on to public roads where they can cause major traffic delays. As with cows and sheep, you can lead them along the public highway as long as you keep them orderly and to one side of the road. Remember, though, that they are easily startled and may be panicked by fast-moving cars or by impatient motorists sounding their horns. It is wise therefore to move them late at night. *Iguanodons* must be awakened very gently: whatever you do, don't ring bells, throw buckets of cold water or shine bright lights in their faces. Treat them as you would a child: shake them gently by the shoulder and quietly murmur something appropriate like, "Time to get up old girl. We're going on a journey." You will probably have to shake and murmur for several minutes.

It is, of course, quite impossible to wake a flock single-handed; by the time even the second one is awake, the first will have squatted down and gone back to sleep. You need a waker for each *Iguanodon*: either hire freelance nightworkers or throw a lavish party. Give your guests just one drink on arrival and, when they are all assembled, explain the procedure – stressing the necessity for a gentle touch. Then lead them out to your pasture and ask each guest to wake an *Iguanodon*. When all the *Iguanodons* are fully awake, the assembled company leads them to their new pasture and returns to your house where you serve more drinks and charcoal-grilled *Iguanodon* steaks.

A prize – often a haunch of *Iguanodon* for the freezer – is awarded to the guest with the most original line in dinosaur pillow talk. Such parties, now known as dinosaur wakes, are becoming hugely popular and many society folk are acquiring herds of *Iguanodon* purely so that they can hold regular dinosaur wakes. The rather clumsy dance of the same name – a cross between a clog dance and a slow polka with the participants wearing Wellington boots and evening dress – originated at dinosaur wakes in Texas.

Suborder Ornithopoda
CAMPTOSAURUS

A straightforward and trouble-free dinosaur for the farmer with plenty of scrub. Fairly manageable but not really suitable for the apartment-dweller.

*C*amptosaurus walks on two legs and grazes on four; it is pleasantly mottled in blues and browns, and is 23 feet long.

Basically it is a grazer but you can't just put a flock in a field and forget about it. It has a horny beak at the front of the mouth, rather like a cow; a long tongue for getting food, like a cow; ridged, closely-packed teeth for crushing and chopping tough vegetation, like a cow; and cheeks which store cropped food and push food between the teeth for grinding, like a cow. Unlike a cow, it cannot digest grass. *Camptosaurus* prefers the leaves of low-growing plants, and the would-be farmer is hard put to it to find an economic food. You *can* use chamomile lawns as food for these dinosaurs, but they are not a realistic solution. Grassland already turning to scrub is a good bet: *Camptosaurus* greedily takes nettles, thistles, brambles, elder, hawthorn and so on

(particularly young plants) and so is useful at clearing weed-infested former pastureland. You will have to move your flock from pasture to pasture fairly frequently. A dinosaur wake (see facing page) is the best method, although there is less social cachet to be obtained from a *Camptosaurus* wake than an *Iguanodon* wake. *Camptosaurus* are usually well-behaved, particularly on public roads at night.

Like so many other things eight yards long, *Camptosaurus* is really for the farmer rather than the apartment-dweller. It is surprising, therefore, that so few farmers have turned to it. The conditions suitable for commercial exploitation of *Plateosaurus* (see pages 46-47) should also be suitable for *Camptosaurus*: in fact, the male of *Camptosaurus* is far more manageable than that of *Plateosaurus* and may be treated like a female. The meat is excellent: very reminiscent of crocodile and rather more tender than *Plateosaurus*; and, because it is scarce it will fetch good prices from the recently established chains of dinosaur butchers.

Breeding is straightforward and trouble-free. Mating occurs in the summer, out in the open. Courtship in cool climates is subtle and inconspicuous, but nevertheless necessary. In warmer climates courtship becomes more florid and may be superfluous. The sexes are not easily distinguished: there is no difference which is easy to see. Use your intuition. Males have a "maleness" that is indefinable but undeniable. A chick is dropped about a year after conception.

If your chick has crooked and weak legs this may be due to a deficiency of calcium (Ca) and Vitamin D (calciferol). Add cod liver oil to the diet and make sure there is plenty of fresh green food available.

Suborder Sauropodomorpha
RIOJASAURUS

Think of this useful prosauropod as the South American equivalent of Plateosaurus (page 46).
It can be profitably farmed there, either like Plateosaurus or free range on the pampas.

To picture this dinosaur all you need do is think of *Plateosaurus* (a stimulating thought indeed!) and then shrink the head somewhat. *Riojasaurus* is the result and it is as profitable a prospect to the Argentine or Peruvian rancher as is *Plateosaurus* to his European counterpart. The fibrous meat lends itself very well to being corned and canned, and it seems likely that *Riojasaurus* will be the third of the three styles of dinoburger – *Iguanodon* and *Camptosaurus* have already been chosen – soon to be launched amid a blaze of publicity (100 *Gallimimus* and a chorus line of *Longisquama* are already in training) by a leading burger chain.

Like *Plateosaurus, Riojasaurus* thrives best under outdoor conditions, but you must provide suitable shelters to which the flock can retire at night or in bad weather. In South America it browses free-range on the pampas, feeding on the local cortaderia during the day. If we can believe Argentine claims, *Riojasaurus* can be trained to return from its pampa to its shelter in the evening by the sound of a horn. On the other hand, claims that the animal can distinguish different arrangements of rhythms and notes, or "tunes", can be discounted: although it has an acute ear, it is not intelligent. An intelligent hadrosaur such as *Parasaurolophus,* on the other hand, itself a producer of many and various noises, might well be trained to respond to a range of tunes, enabling a dinosaur farmer with a sophisticated PA system to live the indolent life of a disc-jockey.

It is a mystery how *Riojasaurus,* with its relatively inefficient teeth and digestive system, manages to survive on a diet as tough as cortaderia. Presumably there are symbiotic bacteria living in the gut which help in the tricky business of digesting this tough reed. If so, it is important that when *Riojasaurus* is ill you do not give it antibiotics, which will kill off these important intestinal flora. Prevention is better than cure: anticipate any health problems. The first signs of ill health may be general and indicate no more than poor husbandry. Unless your dinosaurs are free range, check diet. Try using a different meadow. Bring another of your lakes into use, or a more sheltered hillside. If these measures fail you will have to try a more specific diagnosis and the cure that goes with it. But avoid antibiotics.

Free-range dinosaurs are subject to *Impaction of the Crop*: an obstruction in the crop – coarse grass, hair, feathers – prevents food from entering the stomach. The symptoms are constant belching and you may be able to feel a tell-tale lump in the throat. The best thing to do is inject antiseptic water into the crop.

Suborder Stegosauria
KENTROSAURUS

Here is a stegosaur that is ideal for a farmer with a few square miles of tropical swamp. Almost self-maintaining, Kentrosaurus is easily fed and bred.

Kentrosaurus is a prickly customer about fifteen feet long, with pairs of long spikes attached to the skin of the back and tail, one pair of which juts out sideways at its hips. The first half dozen or so pairs are flattened and have a good blood supply, just as in *Stegosaurus* (page 53). The others are for defence, particularly the ones on the tail which are used as weapons when *Kentrosaurus* wants to drive off real or (more often) assumed enemies. It is amiable but obtuse. If things seem unexpected (and nearly everything that happens is totally unexpected to *Kentrosaurus*) it lashes out.

As in all stegosaurs, feeding can be a problem. Moss-like plants, such as horsetails, and similar soft foods are all that *Kentrosaurus* can manage to chew. The other problem is housing. I should not like to take on the husbandry of *Kentrosaurus* unless I had a dozen or more acres of horsetail-infested swamp, surrounded by a good brick wall at least eight feet high and with an electrically heated, thermostatically controlled, sensibly partitioned enclosure.

This stegosaur catches cold easily and in temperate climates you cannot allow it outside if there is an R in the month, even if the sun is shining. In addition, *Kentrosaurus* is prone to Stegosaur pox. This manifests itself as scabs, lesions of the nose and mouth, a discharge from the mouth and difficulty in breathing. The dinosaur goes off its feed and *looks* ill, with drooping tail and back-spikes. If you detect pox early you may manage to arrest its progress by treating the scabs three times daily with a solution of equal parts of iodine, glycerol and Friar's Balsam. This requires immense care and I suggest the use of an accurate and easily aimed long-range spray. Most modern fire brigades have efficient means of disseminating liquids

and would, I am sure, be extremely happy to advise.

I have already referred to the nervous swipes of its spiky tail. Although *Kentrosaurus* is civil enough and friendly to those it learns to recognize as friends, or even acquaintances, its brain lets it down. Memories fade rapidly, and yesterday's friend is today's menacing stranger. Not even a suit of armour will protect. In your relations with the stegosaurs the golden rule is: do not be intimate. This rule may be bent by hardy farmers in the case of *Scelidosaurus*; but with *Kentrosaurus* (and, of course, *Stegosaurus* itself) it may not.

You might be forgiven for supposing that few dinosaurs are less suitable for meat farming than *Kentrosaurus*. But one man's mite is another man's foison. What we in the developed world find most difficult about *Kentrosaurus* are feeding it and keeping it warm. No such problems are found in the swamps of Central Africa. The Sudd in Sudan, for example, is ideal for stegosaurs: it is one of the largest tropical freshwater swamps in the world and parts could without much difficulty be enclosed and adapted for a flock of *Kentrosaurus*. The climate is ideal for them, food abounds and *Kentrosaurus* flourishes. A further advantage of such a farm is this: stegosaurs will not usually breed in captivity, but this dim dinosaur does not associate such a swamp with captivity, chicks are produced regularly and the size of the flock increases. Once a good-sized flock has built up individuals can be culled as required. Such a farm would almost run itself and would be a boon to the protein-starved third world.

Much of the above applies with equal force to *Scelidosaurus* and *Stegosaurus,* but I think that the future of stegosaur farming in tropical freshwater swamps bounded by mud walls and with labourers' huts on stilts lies first and foremost with *Kentrosaurus*.

Suborder Sauropodomorpha
ANCHISAURUS

*For the farmer who is tempted to try Plateosaurus but unwilling to commit himself
that far, a small dinosaur that can be kept as a pet or reared for meat.*

Although the smaller species are only six feet long and the larger ones only eight feet including the extensive extended tail, in *Anchisaurus* the brontosaur features are present to a full extent. It has short front legs and rather long hind ones. It moves around on its back legs only.

Anchisaurus is one of the most trouble-free and easiest of the prosauropods to keep. Its fault, not admitted universally, is its dullness. It is mild, fairly good-looking, undemanding and very boring. Those who are tempted to see a small *Anchisaurus* as an alternative to *Stegoceras* (page 11) as a companion to take on walks and aeroplanes are advised to forget it. Even though it is different and even though it is found mostly in Connecticut, *Anchisaurus* has absolutely no sense of fun; wherever you take it – on a roller coaster, to the smartest disco, to a film premier or even if you show it a video-tape of the Muppet Show – its expression will remain blank bewilderment.

Better to simply treat it like a goat.

Suborder Sauropodomorpha
PLATEOSAURUS

*Ideal for the professional farmer who is looking for an opportunity to diversify.
Great satisfaction to be gained from getting them to mate successfully.*

Plateosaurus is a large dinosaur which offers opportunities for either profitable use of leisure time or full-time husbandry. It normally walks on all fours, but it stands on its hind legs to reach high vegetation, or when running. It is a social animal, living in herds, and it is massive enough to be warm-blooded. On the thumb and first two fingers are claws: in the cock the thumb claw is very much enlarged and is used in various kinds of sexual encounter (see below).

Plateosaurus has flat teeth and subsists on soft vegetation. In practice this means leaves of shrubs and trees, but not grass. For the average person (but not for the farmer – see below) this may pose expensive problems: he may not have sufficiently extensive non-laurel shrubberies to support even a few *Plateosaurus* (if kept alone, they fail to flourish) together with the small staff needed to maintain a constantly altering landscape; and he may not be able to conjure up sufficient supplies of soft food – silage, cattle feed and so on.

If you have a small lake of a few acres, with plenty of soft, rushy vegetation at the edge, *Plateosaurus* can be kept in an adjacent field and will crop the water plants. The lake must be fenced in because these creatures can swim.

Some individual hens will live happily alone in a field with a herd of domestic cattle or even horses, as long as they are not expected to eat grass; others may not adapt to this circumstance. Flocks of sheep are not useful as companions for plateosaurs.

Plateosaurus could undoubtedly be of some economic importance because it can be kept in fairly large numbers under relatively intense conditions. Although the market for dinosaur meat is still small, it is growing and there can be little doubt that large quantities of meat can be provided by these dinosaurs for little running cost. For the farmer who wishes to start in this profitable field, *Plateosaurus* is an ideal animal for several reasons: at less than twenty feet long, a small flock of females can be kept with only minimal modifications to a traditional cattle farm. Although *Plateosaurus* is a browser rather than a grazer, it is adaptable enough to take the softer grass-based fodders, such as silage and some hays. This may seem expensive, but, in spite of its bulk, *Plateosaurus* is not a big eater and can be kept either near a lake, as mentioned above, or in parkland with shrubs. It must be said, though, that hedges will prove unsuitable for fencing. Electric fences about six feet high are usually effective.

The meat has a pleasing flavour, similar to crocodile and *Camptosaurus* but rather tougher than the latter and therefore less suitable for dinoburgers. It is best either well roasted or well stewed. *Plateosaurus au vin* (use a cut from any leg) and *Ragoût de Plateosaurus* (use the steaks from the rib cage and slice thinly) are just beginning to catch on in fashionable restaurants and clubs in London and New York. A great attraction to butchers is that so many boneless joints – which always fetch high prices – can be cut from a single carcase. Cuts from

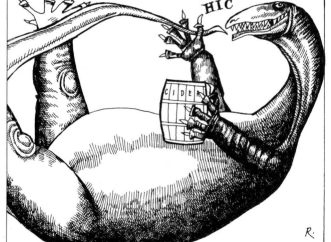

the sirloin are extremely popular, and should be roasted at a low heat, allowing about 50 minutes per pound. Baste regularly and sprinkle with oregano, thyme or rosemary.

Obviously, for breeding, males need to be introduced and here some problems may arise. They are somewhat intractable and difficult to control. The bulk of the male is a disadvantage, and no traditional control method, such as a ring through the nose, has proved wholly suitable. In addition, the greatly enlarged thumb-claw is used as a weapon to no small effect. Dosages of cider have a usefully incapacitating influence and, surprisingly enough, lower the aggressive drive. Beer has a similar effect. When drunk (4-5 gallons are usually sufficient) the male is amiable, though clumsy, and can be led by ropes or cables attached to a neck collar. (His unsteadiness and tendency to fall can cause injury to staff, so it is wise to insure against this.) The main obstacle to breeding under these conditions is that, although the cock is particularly attentive to hens when drunk, successful copulation is very unlikely, in spite of the many, sometimes frenzied, attempts at it that the cock will make. Serious breeders should construct a breeding pen, stoutly built, to which the cider-mellowed cock may be led and confined; when he is sober, hens can be led to him at intervals throughout the day or, if the flock is large, throughout the week. If a series of compartments are constructed, one female can be manoeuvred out while the male's attention is distracted by a new female from the other direction. When mating, the cock needs plentiful supplies of protein in his fodder, particularly nucleo-protein.

Plateosaurus cocks keep their genitalia hidden. This makes the act of mating more of a hit and miss affair than in the familiar mammals. A male *Plateosaurus* has no penis, and total co-operation from the female is therefore essential. In *Plateosaurus* rape is impossible. The cock must to go great lengths to court the hen. The function of courtship here is to bring the hen into a mood not only of acceptance but also of interested participation. The courtship display of the cock, even if you are used to dinosaurs, is impressive. Rearing on his hind legs and swaying from side to side, he inflates a pair of gular sacs on either side of his throat. The skin of these becomes congested with blood due to the dilatation of the blood capillaries there. As a result, the throat becomes both red and large. Meanwhile the male bellows continually (it seems that these air-filled gular sacs act as resonators) at the female. Usually this impressive display results eventually in the female becoming visibly excited, and indicating her willingness to mate. Imperceptive males (particularly the younger ones) may continue to prance and shout. If this continues for too long the female may lose interest

and the whole performance must start again from the beginning. The male uses his thumb claws to get a good grip on his partner. Fertile females have scars on their shoulders; virgins have none.

Males are, on average, bigger than females and it has been suggested that they could be treated as male beef cattle are treated. Castration would, so the argument goes, remove their aggressiveness, and possibly, by making them fatter, cause more forage to be converted into saleable flesh. Unfortunately, many problems attend the castration of dinosaurs. As I have mentioned above, the testes of *Plateosaurus* are internal. Their removal is an operation which, as well as needing considerable surgical skill, entails no small risk to the patient.

Order Pseudosuchia
SALTOPOSUCHUS

A seductive pseudosuchian whose temptations should be resisted by the fond parent looking for a pet. Leave it to the intensive small meat farmer in search of a challenge.

This pseudosuchian differs from its relative *Euparkeria* (page 8) in being fully bipedal; it runs, walks and stands on its hind legs, like a kangaroo. Unlike a kangaroo and in spite of its name, *Saltoposuchus* does not hop or jump. It runs on its toes, balancing with the help of its tail. Its hind legs are much bigger than its front legs, as one might expect, the front legs being used only to grasp food. It is a much more active animal than *Euparkeria*. From the nape of its neck to the tip of its long, powerful tail there are rows of little bony plates protecting its back. *Saltoposuchus* is just as carnivorous as *Euparkeria* and likes plenty of good, meaty food, in large chunks if possible. It seems uninterested in vegetable matter. Try fish. Starlettes and other socially mobile individuals in search of the next smart pet should remain faithful to the phlegmatic *Stegoceras*.

It is relatively small as dinosaurs go – only four feet long – and to that extent fairly manageable, but it is an active predator and not easily tamed, so feeding times present problems. Parents should think twice before deciding to have *Saltoposuchus* as well as children.

Although not yet regularly bred, it is clear that *Saltoposuchus* is essentially a pseudosuchian that should be kept for meat rather than as a pet. Because it is so small it can be intensively farmed rather like mink or fox, and the same sort of diet will do. *Saltoposuchus* will quickly become one of the most sought-after dinosaur meats. It is as tender as lamb and divides neatly into joints. Roast *Saltoposuchus* gives off a mouthwatering aroma and has a succulence reminiscent of roast alligator. The meat makes the very best dinoburgers and steak tartare. In my view *Saltoposuchus* is an excellent proposition for any farmer with a small acreage who is in search of a new goal in life. It is a perfect solution, for example, for the depressed, anxiety-ridden dairy farmer for whom life has become a dull routine.

Plateosaurus is ideally suited to farm life. All it needs is leaves and soft shrubs.

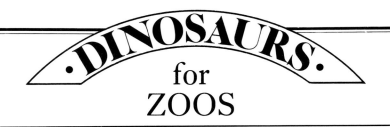

·DINOSAURS· for ZOOS

Order Pseudosuchia
ORNITHOSUCHUS

Not a suitable dinosaur for the amateur; unpredictable, active, predatory and cannibalistic.
For the specialist. Do not be tempted by the chicks: they mature quickly!

It may seem presumptuous for me to advise zoos as to what they may keep. I intend no such patronising slur on their competence of choice: *Ornithosuchus* and the dinosaurs that follow are those that are suitable for keeping only under the excellent and professional conditions found in the larger zoological gardens. Private persons should avoid these. They really should. Some will inevitably ignore this advice. All right, let them try *Ornithosuchus,* which, despite its ability to kill people, is as a young lamb when compared even to *Ceratosaurus* (page 58), let alone that cruel and legendary creature of science fact, *Tyrannosaurus* (page 56).

At nearly ten feet long *Ornithosuchus* is really a bigger, bipedal version of *Euparkeria*. Its back and sides are covered with bony plates, and on the neck these turn into sharp spines. The front of its head is narrow, rather like a beak, and the very powerful jaws are full of sharp teeth. There is a gland on the face, as there is in *Euparkeria*. This seems to be responsible for its musky smell.

Ornithosuchus is a highly predatory carnivore: it needs plenty of meat in large chunks.

Young ones are fairly manageable; a zoo planning to keep more than one in the same enclosure, should make sure that they are the same size. Not for nothing are they protected by bony plates and neck spines: they are very likely to kill and eat smaller and weaker companions, as cannibalism does not perturb them.

Because they are bipedal and warm-blooded they pose a threat to limb and life. The smaller species, about three feet long (half of which is tail), are fairly tractable but may become tricky later on. Females are as bad as males. Keep them permanently behind bars or enclosed with strong wire netting surrounded by a moat.

Ornithosuchus can be bred. Eggs are laid in a crude nest, in sand or light earth. They are scarcely buried and the hen sits on the site; presumably the heat from her body helps to incubate them. She protects the nest against other *Ornithosuchus* and also Man. When the chicks hatch she protects them for a while, then loses interest. After a few days she will eat them if she comes across them. Collect them and rear them yourself.

An ailment called roup often afflicts *Ornithosuchus* and other primitive dinosaurs. It is nearly always due to overcrowding and bad ventilation, and occurs in two forms, one much more serious than the other: (a) *ordinary roup,* when mucus gathers in the mouth; and (b) *diphtheric roup.* This is the more serious one, in which a yellow deposit forms in the back of the throat and the dinosaur frequently sneezes. A mild antiseptic can cure (a) and may help (b). If you catch it early enough (b) may be cured by iodine, glycerol and balsam (see *Kentrosaurus,* page 45).

Croup is either a complication of roup or caused by wounds due to fighting. It is highly contagious and the best remedy is total destruction.

Suborder Stegosauria

SCELIDOSAURUS

Although generally unpopular and a fussy eater, it is a safer, though less spectacular, dinosaur than Stegosaurus (page 53), and should be tried first.

From the start, I must warn you that all the stegosaurs are difficult to feed. They must be kept warm but not too warm, their tempers are uncertain and their reactions often delayed to the point of inertia. But they have a following, small and dedicated. If you are the sort of person who must have a stegosaur, *Scelidosaurus* is the one to start with. It is, at twelve feet long and less than three hundred pounds in weight, more manageable and less delicate than the other stegosaurs. Furthermore, it is not capable of inflicting gross damage to the owner. Sadly, for these reasons alone, the dedicated stegosaurophile is usually less interested in *Scelidosaurus* than in the others, preferring the grotesque unpredictability of the better-known *Stegosaurus*. To those who say, with some justification, that *Scelidosaurus* is an ankylosaur, not a stegosaur, I reply: so what?

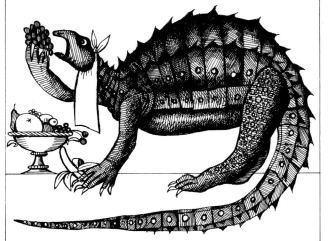

Scelidosaurus is covered by small bony plates embedded in its skin. Some of these are very complicated in shape. It has triangular spikes along the middle of its neck, over its hips and down its tail. Naturally, herbivorous, it is really rather a fussy eater, liking soft vegetables and fruit, but not grass. If you have good access to horsetails, your problems are over. Some – not many – have succeeded with the marsh-loving marestails. Some zoos have succeeded with grain. As grain-eaters swallow their food whole, they need plenty of grit. Charcoal should be added to grit in the ratio 1:20 to ward off flatulence. Automatic seed-hoppers will save labour.

Although I have just described *Scelidosaurus* as unpopular, the adjective was used descriptively rather than pejoratively, as this dinosaur displays the usual stegosaur traits, but in smaller measure. It is finicky with its food, true, but eats less than the other stegosaurs. It needs to be kept warm, certainly, but its size allows you to use a smaller heated cage. I shall not deny that it is stupid and may lash out unexpectedly with its tail, but the likely result is only severe bruising, or at worst a broken leg.

Although *Scelidosaurus* is eminently suitable for zoos, you must remember that most zoos are in cities and the air in cities is polluted. Polluted air may elicit bronchitis; so may poor living conditions, especially cold and damp ones. The symptoms and cure are the same as for asthma (see *Stegoceras*, page 11). Heated Stegosaur houses – similar to elephant houses – are the answer.

I have an unaccountable soft spot for *Scelidosaurus*. It may be because it was born, like me, on the coast of Dorset, that most spell-binding of English counties.

"Lots of cabbages please. I don't like ice cream," says *Stegosaurus*.

Suborder Stegosauria
STEGOSAURUS

Suitable for the well-appointed zoo that has succeeded with Scelidosaurus. Difficult,
delicate and spectacular; sure to draw the crowds. Not for the private individual.

Stegosaurus is nearly thirty feet long and nearly two tons in weight. A series of triangular bony plates is attached to the skin of the back. At the end of the tail are two pairs of spikes, as in *Kentrosaurus* (page 45). It is a spectacular creature, the idea of which, like the idea of *Tyrannosaurus* (page 56) is beloved by children; it is a shame therefore that so few zoos seem able to keep them. They must, of course, be securely enclosed while being permitted plenty of sunlight.

Stegosaurus has two dozen small teeth on each side of the jaw, and cannot eat hard food. However, most individuals can be weaned from their preferred horsetails to other foods. Try deciduous leaves, cow-cake, silage and cabbage. The leaves of beet, carrot, turnip and some orchids (e.g. vanilla) can be offered at appropriate times.

Stegosaurus is the ultimate stegosaur, as you would expect. It is true that it needs heated winter quarters and a cosy dwelling for summer nights. Its great size allows it to put up with cold weather, although it draws the line at frost. Nonetheless, I should not care to take on the husbandry, as opposed to the exhibition, of *Stegosaurus* unless I had the sort of fortified swamp which I recommended for the smaller *Kentrosaurus* (page 45).

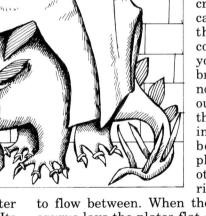

Stegosaurus has a high metabolism (someone has calculated that it has the highest metabolism/brain-weight ratio in the animal kingdom!) which allows it to wander about in cool weather and reach latitudes other Stegosaurs cannot reach. You may think that this is a snag in hot weather, but *Stegosaurus* has an almost unique cooling device. The bony plates on its back are covered with skin and are well supplied with blood vessels. In hot weather the plates stand up vertically on its back and the blood supply to the capillaries on the surface is increased. By this means heat carried by the blood from the body radiates away, cooling the stegosaur. As you can see at a glance, the broadest part of the plate is not nearest the base, but about a third of the way up, so that the most effective cooling is some way from the body. Furthermore, the plates are not opposite each other, but alternate left and right, allowing air currents to flow between. When the weather is cold, *Stegosaurus* lays the plates flat on their sides on its sides and cuts down the blood supply, so that heat is lost far more slowly. The ears of the elephant fulfil a similar function, though far less efficiently. Conversely, when *Stegosaurus* is cooler than the outside world, perhaps in mid-morning, the dorsal plates may absorb radiant energy from the sun.

Order Pseudosuchia
ERYTHROSUCHUS

This pseudosuchian is essentially for the specialist collector. It is unmanageable, intractable and susceptible to gut disorders. Leave it to the zoo.

This is a large, stout, short-tailed, heavy-limbed, high-faced creature, which usually grows to about thirteen feet in length. Although it is not aquatic, in appearance it is not unlike a large crocodile; its skull is about three feet long. It seems a little clumsy, but as it is big and eats meat, its surprising turn of speed should be borne in mind by prospective owners. This is the sort of animal that zoos acquire only in order to enlarge their collection. Unless it is the only dinosaur in a zoo, it will not pull the crowds. Private collectors, unless they are veteran lion-tamers depressed by the routine of their jobs, should keep *Erythrosuchus* firmly in its outdoor cage at all times.

Erythrosuchus is carnivorous, but will accept carrion, fish and other high-protein food. Twice weekly feedings will be sufficient. Be careful not to give it moldy, contaminated or stale food (particularly during hot weather), or water in which soft food has been allowed to ferment. This may lead to enteritis. Enteritis is not to be confused with diarrhoea: dinosaur enteritis is actually inflammation of the mucous membrane of the gut. Be that as it may, the symptoms of enteritis and diarrhoea are the same: the droppings are very fluid, copious and green-tinted, and are almost always foul-smelling. The sick dinosaur has a poor appetite and excessive thirst.

Here is the cure: take the animal into a warm, even temperature of 85°F. If the skin is fouled, use a gentle jet from a hose to wash with disinfectant and warm water (be careful!). Do not forget the feet and legs, and clean the vent with a soft brush (be very careful!). Observe hygiene strictly. For one week add ½ lb powdered catachu, 2 oz powdered calcium phenol sulphate, 2 oz powdered sodium phenol sulphate, 4 oz powdered zinc sulphate to every gallon of drinking water. If you find it difficult to raise the temperature of its living quarters to 85°F, use a hospital cage: you will need a box cage with a *glass* front (armoured if possible), which can be artificially heated.

Suborder Ceratopia
TRICERATOPS

To the zoo with wide open spaces big enough for a flock, Triceratops will bring all the atmosphere of the Wyoming Upper Cretaceous.

The horned and frilled dinosaurs, of which *Triceratops* is the best-known example, are the most advanced dinosaurs in the sense that they were the last to evolve. It is a pity that most of them are too big to be kept conveniently by the man in the street. *Protoceratops* (page 33) and *Leptoceratops* (page 13) are exceptions, of course.

Triceratops is infinitely tempting, I know, but should really be left to those zoos which can give it plenty of well-enclosed space. If you cannot resist having a go with one of the bigger ceratopians, *Pachyrhinosaurus* is a challenge that can sometimes be met (see page 64).

All the ceratopians but *Leptoceratops* are quadrupeds. Of these, all but *Protoceratops* are large quadrupeds. They have very big heads and beaks. All of them have immense frills of bone protecting the neck and shoulders, although these may not be particularly conspicuous. Each of them except *Pachyrhinosaurus* has at least one long horn, and usually three, on its head. The sharp, horny beak, usually used to chop up food, can also be used to chop up enemies.

Because their brains are small, and it may take them weeks or months to sort out their friends from their enemies, the ceratopians need specially careful treatment: they can cause problems.

A description of *Triceratops* itself will make some of these problems manifest. Its beautiful proportions may prevent you from appreciating the sheer size of the creature. Do not, please, think of it as a sort of rhinoceros. A big male is thirty-six feet long and more than twice the size of a fully grown rhinoceros!

The head appears to make up a third of the total length, but most of this is not really part of the true head region. A great frill of bone projects from the skull back over the neck nearly to the shoulders. As well as being a useful defensive shield, particularly against other males and predators such as *Tyrannosaurus*, this bone acts as an attachment area for the enormous muscles of the jaws and neck. Two large horns protrude over the eyes, and an-

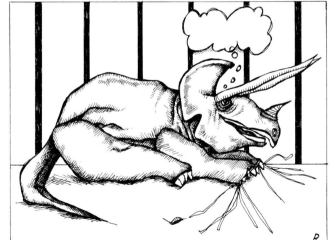

other over the nose. Its jaws contain neat and narrow rows of numerous teeth which work like scissors, and it has a strong and sharp horny beak. When it chooses to, *Triceratops* can gallop.

With this formidable feeding apparatus, *Triceratops* can deal with almost any vegetable material and prefers fibrous and juicy plants such as young palms and giant rhubarb. Plant its enclosures with giant redwood, maidenhair, poplar, oak, and maple. You must make very large quantities available.

Although you can keep *Triceratops* in small groups, or even singly, there is no denying that it will really flourish only in a largish flock. In such a group the instinctive flock dominance hierarchy (FDH) manifests itself and the keeper's personal relationships with individual *Triceratops,* difficult at the best of times, become submerged by the various innate flock-structure maintenance behaviours (IFSMBs). More simply put, if a male thinks that you are another, the FDH part of the IFSMB will preponderate and may, by a process of social facilitation, propagate itself. Every organism ecphorizes the inherited engrams of its origin. As a result, you may find two dozen ten-ton animals galloping at you head down, yard-long horns foremost, at 30 mph.

As you might have gathered, the males fight each other in spring and early summer, which is their mating season. Rivals face each other, bellowing and alternately bowing and tossing their massive heads, showing their opponents their horns and shields. Usually matters proceed no further. The smaller or weaker male moves off. But if the two are evenly matched they will fight, ramming each other head on. These battles often result in severe wounds, but deaths are rare.

With individual specimens of *Triceratops* some form of mutual affection can build up. It is not an intelligent dinosaur and it may mistake you for someone else. As it is bulky, beaked and horned, this may lead to an irreversible conclusion.

Suborder Theropoda
TYRANNOSAURUS

The ultimate animal for the zoo with dwindling attendances. Literally awful and almost certainly needing a special insurance policy. By far the least suitable carnosaur to keep.

With *Tyrannosaurus* we reach the end of the line – the biggest and most formidable of the carnivorous dinosaurs. Forty feet long, seventeen feet high and weighing more than seven tons, *Tyrannosaurus* is a machine for killing other dinosaurs. Its head is four feet long and holds a battery of saw-edged teeth six inches long. Its main weapons are the massive hind feet which bear talons eight inches long. Its front legs are tiny and not used in catching or killing its prey: they are used to help *Tyrannosaurus* to get up when it has been lying down. They are supported by massive shoulder muscles. The claws on them are used as toothpicks!

Tyrannosaurus usually walks slowly and ponderously with its body held horizontally and in what has been described as a swan-neck curve for flexibility. The surprisingly short, but stiff and heavy, tail is raised off the ground as a counterweight. Although it seems clumsy and pigeon-toed, *Tyrannosaurus* is capable of moving more quickly in short bursts.

In the wild, *Tyrannosaurus* hunts in flocks and is less likely to kill its companions than is *Ceratosaurus*. Although the principles of carnosaur husbandry are set out under *Ceratosaurus* (page 58), you need to remember the extra problems involved in the management of a flock of half a dozen forty-foot carnivorous dinosaurs: space, feeding and, these days, insurance. That said, it is only when kept in flocks that *Tyrannosaurus* will breed. For maximum security and minimum premiums, I suggest that around your *Tyrannosaurus* pit you build something akin to the Berlin Wall, and that watch be kept around the clock by sentries equipped with searchlights and rockets. The public can view from the top of such a wall and from walkways suspended high above the pit. Cage in all viewing points or your zoo will almost certainly be the scene of some spectacular murders. The chicks are about three feet long at birth and weigh about fifteen pounds. But *think* before you take a little baby home with you. Will it be quite as cuddly in a year's time?

Suborder Theropoda
SPINOSAURUS

This ponderous and brutal Egyptian giant is suitable only for the best-appointed and most security-conscious zoos. It needs a lot of heat and special care.

This carnosaur is thirty-nine feet long, more than twice the length of *Ceratosaurus,* and it also walks on its hind legs. Its front legs are unexpectedly strong: the largest carnosaurs, like *Tyrannosaurus,* usually have tiny front legs. The unique feature of *Spinosaurus* is the "sail" on its back, supported by six-foot-long spines on the vertebrae, which has a very efficient blood supply and acts as a heat exchanger. When too warm, *Spinosaurus* cools itself by radiating heat away through the sail; in the cool early morning it warms itself by holding the sail at right angles to the rising sun. In temperate countries you must give it warmth and ultra-violet spotlights.

Don't worry! There's a deep pit between *Tyrannosaurus* and those people.

Suborder Theropoda
CERATOSAURUS

If your zoo needs a carnosaur, Ceratosaurus, the smallest of them, is the one to choose. It is beyond the scope of even the biggest private collectors.

C eratosaurus is a carnosaur. All the carnosaurs are carnivores, and none has much discrimination in any relevant aspect (relevant, that is to say, to man). They are all bipedal; all have huge jaws supplied with horrid teeth; all have huge feet armed with horrid claws; all will kill and eat anything that moves; all have proved to be treacherous and fatal friends, even when hand-reared from the egg. I cannot recommend any of them as a pet, even *Ceratosaurus* which, at only eighteen feet long and one or two tons in weight, is the smallest one. *Ceratosaurus* is otherwise distinguished by a bony spike on its snout and a bony knob above each eye. These are used, as we shall see later, in battles of sexual rivalry between males.

How can even a big zoo cope with carnosaurs? There must be massively secure, centrally-heated pits, and a capacity to supply the meat that will be needed. A useful rule of thumb for quantity is one duck per day per ten-foot length. Two ducks a day is sufficient for a full-grown *Ceratosaurus*. For the larger carnosaurs you can start thinking in terms of geese, pigs, donkeys, horses, cattle, wildebeeste and so on. I recommend a routine of feast and fast, the fasts lasting for at least a fortnight. I hesitate, for obvious reasons, to recommend the eggs of other dinosaurs, but there is

no doubt that *Ceratosaurus* does particularly appreciate the addition of this luxury to its diet. Otherwise, very large numbers of birds' eggs are desirable: chickens' eggs are probably best and certainly the cheapest. Protoceratops' eggs can be reserved for birthdays.

Male *Ceratosaurus* tend to fight one another. In the wild such sexual sparring is ritualized into a head-butting routine in which neither of the contestants is seriously hurt. When one of the rivals recognizes the superior strength of his opponent he stops the butting and runs away. The winner, no longer stimulated to attack by the sight of another male, ignores the loser. Do not be misled by this into supposing that you can keep two males in one pit. The vanquished cock, prevented from escape by the walls of the pit, is unable to avoid the victor, who will attack him without mercy, not only with the top of his head, but also with his teeth and the sharp claws of his hind feet. There can be only one outcome: the death of a dinosaur. You may be tempted to keep a cock with a hen, hoping for the arrival of chicks. Resist temptation: a cock will kill a hen, not out of malice, but in passing. What about a small flock of hens? Again, this is not worth risking: sooner or later, in the necessarily enclosed conditions of captivity, one will be killed and eaten, then another and so on until only one remains.

·DINOSAURS· for SAFARI PARKS

Suborder Sauropodomorpha
DICRAEOSAURUS

A realistic first brontosaur for your stately safari park: given sufficient space and housing,
easily kept and satisfactorily fertile if proper precautions are taken.

Most of the dinosaurs that might be used in safari parks are brontosaurs. However, people have failed more often with brontosaurs, despite their familiar long-necked, long-tailed appearance, than with any other group of dinosaurs. This failure has been due almost entirely to ignorance – ignorance reinforced by published error. This error concerns brontosaur ecology and has naturally affected the ways in which people have tried to look after them. Before we can start to think about brontosaur culture, we must abort one misconception, namely that brontosaurs are swamp-dwellers. *Brontosaurs are terrestrial.* They do not live in water and will survive (in the wild) without entering water for days on end. From this error, still promulgated by books on dinosaurs, even textbooks on dinosaurs, follows another: brontosaurs do not eat fish, molluscs or crustaceans and are not even very fond of soft water-weeds. Their preferred diet is leaves, buds, soft branches and fruit.

Once emancipated from received falsehood, the keen brontosaurist can begin to succeed. For, though it may not seem sensible, many men must make the attempt to keep the biggest land animals of all simply because, like mountains, they are there. Here lies the problem – the sheer scale of the creatures is difficult to grasp. The problem is compounded by the fact that brontosaurs must live in flocks to be happy. Space is at a premium. For this reason alone, if you must keep brontosaurs, I

recommend that you should start with *Dicraeosaurus.* At only forty-two feet long and ten feet high it is the brontosaur with which you are most likely to succeed. It is the usual brontosaur shape, with tail held out stiffly to counterbalance the long neck. In colour it is brontosaur grey, the young being rather darker. As in all brontosaurs, its intelligence is negligible and its food vegetable.

Dicraeosaurus is undiscriminating. If you really have fifty acres or so of parkland with strong fencing, keeping and displaying this brontosaur to the public is feasible in the summer. In the winter, except in the tropics, feeding, housing and putting on view are big problems. Five or six hundredweight of vegetation per *Dicraeosaurus* per day is needed. Fortunately, most vegetable matter is accepted.

When all danger of frost has passed, *Dicraeosaurus* can be kept outside in its park or scrubland provided that it is well fenced. You will need stout metal palings: although electric fencing is tempting and usually effective, a shocked brontosaur can twitch violently, breaking the electric wire and allowing the entire flock to escape into the countryside. The damage caused by a flock on the loose must be reckoned in five or six figures and will have to be borne by you, the owner. You must also bear in mind the damage almost certainly suffered by the animals. *Dicraeosaurus* is a member of a noticeably unintelligent group of dinosaurs and has difficulty, I think it is fair to say, with all

Watch out young man! That *Dicraeosaurus* has got his eye on you.

man-made objects. It will walk into walls, high-tension cables, streetlamps, hot dog stands, cathedrals and so on, to mutual detriment.

Housing in winter raises enormous problems – of space and heat in particular. Converted airship hangars seem to be the best bet. Brontosaurs are sufficiently social to need company indoors, so a series of smaller buildings is not the answer. Nor can individually heated pens be recommended, for the same reason. A lonely brontosaur becomes an unhealthy brontosaur. What you need is a building large enough to contain, with space to move about, a dozen or more animals, each – in the case of the larger brontosaur species – at least half the length of a football field, and containing facilities for regular feeding at a height of about seven or eight feet from the floor. As far as the floor itself is concerned, there must be facilities for mucking out at least twice a day. You can keep the manure (indeed you would be foolish not to) and use it to fertilize the summer feeding grounds. You can also, if you prefer, bag it and sell it to gardeners and farmers. It is, for dinosaur dung, relatively inoffensive.

Breeding, unexpectedly, is not much of a problem either. Provided that a largish flock is kept with plenty of space (about eight acres per hen) eggs will be laid from time to time without any participation being required of you. Young hatch in early summer and can run around actively after a few minutes. The chicks are short-necked and relatively short-tailed. They are not likely to graze, even if grass is there, but will happily crop away at low shrubs or bushes. Roses are a favourite (though hybrid teas, curiously, are rejected).

When there are chicks the flock organizes itself in such a way that the young are protected. In times of danger, whether real or not, the chicks gather in a bunch and are surrounded by a ring of females. The male brontosaurs roam around the edge of the ring, trying to identify the source of danger and then charging at it in an uncomprehending and comprehensive way. This is dangerous to man in the same way that an earthquake is dangerous to man: the danger is random, because a male *Dicraeosaurus* (or any male brontosaur, for that matter) does not as a rule associate a tiny man-sized figure with danger and treads on him only by mistake. That said, it must be added that the *Dicraeosaurus,* the smallest brontosaur, is the one most likely to recognize a man as a possible predator and to make a real effort to beat him flat. The keeper should be a small man or woman.

Once brontosaurs learn to recognize someone (a process that may, unfortunately, take some months), they will tolerate his presence among them, even close to the chicks, which can then be fed individually if necessary. After prolonged exposure, a herd of brontosaurs will become accustomed to people and motor vehicles. However, there is still a high risk of cars being crushed by mistake, and safari park proprietors must either run a securely fenced road through the enclosure or provide special crush-proof vehicles. A road should disappear into a tunnel from time to time so that the brontosaurs can cross freely above it. Owners who wish to display their brontosaurs in the winter must provide electrically-powered transport – a narrow gauge electric railway is best – so as to avoid the accumulation of fumes.

Suborder Sauropodomorpha
APATOSAURUS

*For an enormous enclosed acreage, the most brontosaurian dinosaur of all. With a lake
in summer and warmth in winter, a flock will give you an enviable reputation.*

A patosaurus can be considered about as typical a brontosaur as it is possible to get, with a tiny head, a long neck and a long tail. It will draw the crowds as well as any, apart from the elegant *Diplodocus* and, of course, the giant *Brachiosaurus*. Buns, ice creams and most of the food that children throw out of cars will not harm it. Treat it just as you would any other brontosaur: with respect.

As well as at least a hundred acres of parkland and scrub, a substantial lake must be provided for mating. The same precautions must be taken when admitting the public as for *Dicraeosaurus* (page 59). If you do have an emergency – say *Apatosaurus* picks up a child by the collar – you can play on the brontosaur's immense gullibility to retrieve the situation. At the sight of a large carnosaur – *Tyrannosaurus* is ideal – they will drop everything and run. Even though they never encounter *Tyrannosaurus* in the wild, they sense danger. Fortunately you do not need a real *Tyrannosaurus* to frighten a brontosaur: keep a life-size model at the ready – an inflatable will do as long as you always keep it fully inflated – and wheel it into view as soon as the crisis occurs. Your insurance company will appreciate this.

Being sixty-five feet long, *Apatosaurus* finds copulation difficult under normal gravitational conditions;

the problem is usually solved by the buoyancy provided by water. The males and females splash into the water together. They are competent swimmers, and the unconstraining discipline of an aqueous medium together with the stimulating presence of large numbers of their flock arouses desire and provokes them to courtship ("pre-coital activity" is a clumsier but more accurate description of what goes on). Mating in the brontosaurs is more prosaic than poetic, although there is an epic quality. In sharp contrast to the dinosaurs we have so far dealt with, the male *Apatosaurus* has a penis. This helps copulation, but does not make it easy. The total cooperation of the female is needed and many hours of courtship by the male are required to convince her that it is a good idea to respond to his thirty-ton gambollings and stentorian bellowings by coiling her neck and tail about his. This stage reached, coitus is a formality. Like other formal occasions it may last a long time, but is usually over by sundown. Passion wanes as the water cools. Five or so oval eggs are laid in spring.

In winter, warmth is required for the flock, particularly at night. I cannot begin to make suggestions, beyond emphasizing the importance of an enormous enclosed acreage of the type I have described under *Dicraeosaurus* (page 59).

Suborder Sauropodomorpha
CAMARASAURUS

Camarasaurus is delightful, charming and full of character. Ideal material for someone moving into brontosaur-keeping who has cut his teeth on Dicraeosaurus.

I n my opinion, of all the brontosaurs, *Camarasaurus* is the one of which you could most truly say that it possesses a character. Some describe the chicks as "delightful" and "charming", and so they are. But they do grow up, and with maturity comes a psychological need for the flock. When kept in a flock their charm and individuality are submerged in the group's collective unconscious. Kept alone, they pine and wane.

However, if you can manage to extricate two or three very young – three to four weeks old – *Camarasaurus* from the flock and exhibit them in a small paddock, you will draw huge crowds of children and their parents who will find the creatures' playful fighting and the squeaky noise they make hugely amusing. Seasoned entrepreneurs will surround this paddock with souvenir shops, refreshment halls, beer tents, carousels and roller coasters. Detaching the young from the flock is best accomplished by a skilled exponent of lasso, or lariat, working from an armoured car driven by a movie stuntman. Return the young to the flock before they are two months old. If you are lucky and have a large enough flock, you will have young of the right age throughout the summer.

Suborder Sauropodomorpha
DIPLODOCUS

This is one of the longest dinosaurs, a graceful brontosaur for the connoisseur. When you have succeeded with the others, but not until then, try one.

A lthough *Diplodocus* is, at eighty-five feet, a very long dinosaur, thirty-nine of those feet are tail and twenty-four neck. It is a slender, almost delicate brontosaur and has a thumb-claw for mating. It is not stretching affection too far, I think, to describe it as graceful, even beautiful. It is therefore especially suitable for the upper end of the safari park market: those parks which were landscaped – probably centuries ago – by a master and where the visitor, on emerging from a clump of ancient oak or beech, is presented with a vista which uplifts his careworn twentieth-century heart – perhaps magnolia and rhododendron in the foreground, a rolling lawn, a lake, a discreet waterfall, some elegant pines strewn here and there, some thistle-filled meadows and a distant tree-covered hillside – the sort of scene which you might think it impossible to enhance, but to which a pair of *Diplodocus,* quietly browsing in the middle distance, add something difficult to define but nonetheless real and powerful. It has to do with the element of time. The realization that these noble creatures have been living their simple pastoral existence in such a place and in such a manner for 190 million years gives the twentieth-century visitor an insight – at once humbling and uplifting – into the essential unchangeability of life on Earth.

Treat like other brontosaurs, but make allowances. *Diplodocus* is dim-witted even by brontosaur standards. Fragile, beautiful and massively stupid: a combination that has appealed to man since Adam.

Suborder Sauropodomorpha
BRACHIOSAURUS

As the largest land animal in the world, this is the Everest of dinosaur keeping.
Problems abound but it is a challenge that the bravest will want to accept.

U p to now this has always been considered the largest dinosaur, although the apparent availability of so-called *"Supersaurus"* in the Colorado area shows us that even dinosaurs are being "promoted" these days.

Brachiosaurus is, at more than seventy feet in length and eighty tons (for the statistically-minded, the weight of sixteen elephants), the largest land animal so far. It is not the usual brontosaur shape as its front legs are much longer than its hind ones; with neck stretched up it can be up to forty feet high. It is the most upright of the brontosaurs, and its head has a more distinguished look than the other brontosaurs, with nostrils on the top on a little lump. Its tail is relatively short, of course, in obedience to the Principle of Moments (the neck being characteristically more often more vertical than in the other brontosaurs). It is an awesome animal, and if you succeed with it, your name will become household and your flock of brachiosaurs a living legend.

In its care and culture *Brachiosaurus* needs what *Dicraeosaurus* needs, only more of it: space, food and warmth. Most brontosaur winter quarters pose immense problems. Those of *Brachiosaurus* pose immense problems to those dinosaur keepers who have solved the problems posed by the other brontosaurs. If you are looking for a crumb of comfort, you may find it in the fact that a large lake is not strictly necesary for the health of *Brachiosaurus*. A pond of perhaps an acre or two will be sufficient for the summer, and a heated running stream, say six feet wide and six feet deep, flowing through the winter quarters should help tide the flock over the dark months of winter. If you are economically-minded, you may be able to arrange a system of sluices and dams whereby this stream may be diverted over the floor to help in the cleansing of the house (the so-called Augean solution).

Brachiosaurus is by no means as easy to breed as some of the other brontosaurs. In Tanzania both sexes are brought into heat by simulated rain.

Suborder Ceratopia
PACHYRHINOSAURUS

Perhaps the most suitable of the frilled dinosaurs for the safari park. Treat
like a rhino and keep vehicles away from maverick males.

A lthough you will always hear people suggesting that ceratopians (the horned and frilled dinosaurs) are ideal for safari parks, I cannot wholly agree. *Protoceratops* (page 33) and *Leptoceratops* (page 13) are the only really suitable ceratopians for the ordinary man. However, *Pachyrhinosaurus* is at least a likely possibility for the well-

stocked safari park. This large dinosaur has no horns and is equipped instead with a thick, bony lump between its eyes, hollowed out like a crater. You can keep *Pachyrhinosaurus* under the same sorts of conditions that you would keep a White Rhinoceros.

Males sometimes butt vehicles that enter their paddocks. Little damage is done to the dinosaur.

"Not another one wanting me to smile! If only I had the stomach for meat," thinks *Brachiosaurus*.

Suborder Pterodactylia
QUETZALCOATLUS

The largest flying animal, easily fed but not so easily housed. A drive-through desert safari park
could be modified, though not cheaply, to display this majestic Texan pterosaur.

L ogically, as a pterosaur, *Quetzalcoatlus* should be included under "Flying Pets" (page 16), but its great size makes it suitable only for a very large safari park. With a wing span of thirty-five feet or more, it dwarfs even *Pteranodon* (page 69). It is as delicate in build as *Pteranodon,* too, but (except for its black neck and head) covered with black fur. It will certainly attract the crowds.

Its food is carrion: you should feed it any very dead animals or parts of animals.

Unlike *Pteranodon, Quetzalcoatlus* will survive for years in captivity, although it doesn't flourish. It relies wholly on thermal air currents to keep it aloft and is found, therefore, in hot deserts, where such vertical winds are characteristic. Horizontal winds are a danger to such a delicately built creature. In hot, windless weather it can be seen soaring high in the sky, wheeling and circling with effortless grace, scanning the ground for corpses. Vultures scatter at the merest hint of this exquisite scavenger.

It is clear that only a few safari parks will be suitable, and these for only some of the time. What are the characteristics of a park suitable for *Quetzalcoatlus*? First, it must be situated in a hot desert; second, the desert must be windless. It need not be hot all the time, nor windless all the time, but there should be enough sun to produce the thermals required to support the gliding *Quetzalcoatlus* and sufficient windless days for tourists to have a good chance of seeing *Quetzalcoatlus* soaring above their heads without the creature risking damage by unexpected gusts. For a safari park to justify its description the animals in it must be free-ranging, at least within the confines of their enclosure: onlookers must enter their enclosure in order to view them. A permanently caged *Quetzalcoatlus* is a sorry sight. But if it's allowed to fly, how can you prevent the escape of your pterosaur?

The best, and perhaps only, method is to build a high "cage" around a site of at least fifty acres (two hundred and fifty acres would be better). String netting, as used in ships' rigging, attached firmly to the ground and held taut at the other end by helium-filled balloons is the cheapest method. Check netting regularly for signs of *Quetzalcoatlus* trying to escape. A height of ten thousand feet should be enough. Although *Quetzalcoatlus* may soar higher than this in the wild, if you feed it well it doesn't need to fly high; indeed, it will probably not fly at all, preferring to hang up somewhere, upside-down in typical pterosaur fashion. Your feeding regime should therefore steer between surfeit and starvation: feed it when it begins to fly above naked eyesight.

Suborder Theropoda
STRUTHIOMIMUS

An extremely fast two-legged runner, Struthiomimus really needs the wide open spaces provided by a park. Easily fed and cared for. No landed gentry should be without a flock.

Struthiomimus is a very ostrich-like dinosaur, with a toothless, horny beak. With its long tail stiffened as a counterbalance to its long neck, it is very like *Ornithomimus* (page 25), but has heavy, ursine claws at the ends of its fingers.

Its diet is similar to that of *Ornithomimus,* but it is much more herbivorous: eggs, fruit, branches. In fact its diet is not unlike that of the ostrich and very little is refused. Give it a small mammal or lizard for a treat.

If you have kept *Ornithomimus* and been charmed, *Struthiomimus* offers an extension of the experience. No larger than *Ornithomimus, Struthiomimus* is more specialized. It is faster on the straight (up to 50 mph), and should only be ridden by those who have completely mastered *Ornithomimus.* It needs to be kept in flocks to flourish, and, as you can appreciate, it needs enclosures of several acres in area. If it has enough space it will develop its own social organization, the flock having its own recognized pecking order. This social structure is relatively rigid and family groups soon separate out, after some initial sparring between the bigger males. Once a pair has formed and chicks are born (born, not laid) the family sticks together in a sub-group within the flock, with the father as dominant animal. Curiously enough, in the flock as a whole the leader or dominant dinosaur, is as often as not a female – usually a widow, but rarely an old maid.

Harmless to tourists.

Suborder Sauropodomorpha
MASSOSPONDYLUS

This elegant prosauropod is an impressive addition to any safari park, where it is easily fed and accommodated; gentle, but too big to wander among pedestrians.

At nearly fourteen feet long, *Massospondylus* approaches the sort of size on which the reputation of dinosaurs largely rests. It is closely related to *Thecodontosaurus* (page 10) and resembles it in shape.

Much the same sort of food should be given to *Massospondylus* as to *Thecodontosaurus,* although the former is more of a vegetarian and is therefore, in spite of its greater size, little more expensive to maintain – in summer at least – if kept outside in a roomy paddock with plenty of shrubs. It prefers rose bushes above all else and this can be a nuisance, but many individuals will adapt fairly happily to brambles.

Although it won't draw the crowds like some of the large brontosaurs, it is popular with safari park proprietors because of its manageability, and popular with their visitors because of its friendliness. It will lumber up to parked cars and peer in at the windows. This is quite safe as long as the windows are kept closed, and provides excellent opportunities for home movie and video enthusiasts. If you find one standing in the middle of the road, you may be in for a long wait. It is not deaf, simply unmoved by the sound of car horns. Just sit tight, get your camera ready and wait until the line of traffic reaches back to the park entrance; a keeper will arrive and move the animal by offering it roses.

Whoops! You didn't see *Pteranodon* coming, did you? That's because he's white all over.

·DINOSAURS· that are NOT RECOMMENDED

Suborder Pterodactylia
PTERANODON

In these conservation-minded times, it would be irresponsible indeed to recommend the captivity of one of our most beautiful and delicate pterosaurs.

P teranodon is the best of the bunch, in some people's eyes, and I'm not sure that I don't go along with them, at least some of the way. It has a wing span of more than twenty-five feet, a body length of nine or ten feet and a head more than six feet long. This suggests mass, but *Pteranodon* weighs only twenty to thirty pounds. Covered with pure white fur, *Pteranodon* is titanic thistledown.

Why is it white? We don't yet know why it is white all over, but we do know why the head and underparts are covered with white fur: camouflage. *Pteranodon* feeds on fish; fish are less likely to see an aerial predator if its underside is white than if it is any other colour.

In the wild, *Pteranodon* floats on air currents from the waves and cliffs of its natural seashore habitat. It catches fish by using its immense beak, and stores these, pelican-like, in its throat-pouch. The enormous bony crest that extends behind the beak balances the head, and is used for steering and stabilizing. *Pteranodon* is not massively muscular, but its thin-walled bones are filled with air so that its enormous wingspan can keep it in the air without the need for flapping its wings, like the albatross.

Pteranodon nests in colonies on the tops of cliffs. The female lays very small eggs and these are incubated by both parents in turn. The young are helpless when newly hatched and are carefully looked after by the adults, who protect and feed them. While one of the parents remains on the nest incubating the naked young, the other flies out to sea, catches fish and returns to the nest. When its beak is pecked by one of the babies, pieces of half-digested fish are regurgitated into the pouch; the babies reach in and gobble them up. When the time comes, the young launch themselves from the top of the cliff into space. They fly without any practice at all and try to fish like the adults, although until they learn skilled fishing methods they fly home to be fed by their parents.

Many young perish in their first year. Some, landing on the water, are unable to take off again, and drown. In some, the single, elongated finger bone that supports the wing-membrane may be broken in the rough and tumble of the cliff-top colony, or the membrane itself may tear. In either case death from starvation or predation (pterosaurs are cannibals) is inevitable.

No beast so large and delicate can be kept successfully in the necessary bounds of captivity. No enclosure can provide it with the conditions it needs, and attempts to keep it always result in an unhappy, unhealthy *Pteranodon,* wasting away to an inevitable death. Unlike many pterosaurs they cannot be released in the hope that they will return to the owner. They float away, never to return.

Enough said: they won't breed in captivity. If you manage to hatch the eggs yourself the young won't thrive and will scarcely ever reach maturity. Leave them be.

CLASSIFICATION OF DINOSAURS

Systematists differ in their ideas of dinosaur classification. Although not approved by all palaeontologists, this scheme will help you to see where your dinosaur fits in. All the dinosaurs recommended in this book are listed in the table that follows. The numerals in the classification column refer to the numerals on the classification scheme. Dinosaurs are dated by the strata in which they are found. The Triassic spans 225 to 193 million years ago; the Jurassic 193 to 136 million years ago and the Cretaceous, 136 to 65 million years ago.

SUPERCLASS	Endosauropsida
CLASS	Pterosauria — Dinosauria
ORDER	Rhamphorhyncia (1) Pterodactylia (2) — Ornithischia Saurischia Aves (1) Pseudosuchia (2)
SUBORDER	Ornithopoda (3) Ceratopia (4) Stegosauria (5) Ankylosauria (6) Theropoda Sauropodomorpha
INFRAORDER	Coelurosauria (7) Deinonychosauria (8) Carnosauria (9) Prosauropoda (10) Sauropoda (11)

CLASSIFICATION	GENUS	AGE	WHERE FOUND	LENGTH (feet)	DIET	PAGE
Dinosauria 1	Archaeopteryx	Jurassic	Germany	2	Carnivorous	16
,, 2	Euparkeria	Triassic	South Africa	2-3	Carnivorous	8
,, 2	Podopteryx	Triassic	Kirgizstan, USSR	⅔	Omnivorous	7
,, 2	Scleromochlus	Triassic	Europe	3	Carnivorous	26
,, 2	Longisquama	Triassic	Turkestan, USSR	3	Omnivorous	36
,, 2	Ornithosuchus	Triassic	Europe	10	Carnivorous	50
,, 2	Erythrosuchus	Triassic	South Africa	14	Carnivorous	54
,, 2	Saltoposuchus	Triassic	Europe	4	Carnivorous	48
,, 3	Fabrosaurus	Triassic	South Africa	3	Herbivorous	10
,, 3	Heterodontosaurus	Triassic	South Africa	3	Herbivorous	13
,, 3	Stegoceras	Cretaceous	North America	6	Herbivorous	11
,, 3	Hypsilophodon	Cretaceous	England	4	Herbivorous	32
,, 3	Camptosaurus	Jurassic	North America, England	23	Herbivorous	43
,, 3	Iguanodon	Cretaceous	Europe	35	Herbivorous	42
,, 3	Anatosaurus	Cretaceous	North America	30	Herbivorous	34
,, 3	Parasaurolophus	Cretaceous	North America	32	Herbivorous	35
,, 3	Psittacosaurus	Cretaceous	Mongolia	8	Herbivorous	32
,, 4	Leptoceratops	Cretaceous	North America	6	Herbivorous	13
,, 4	Protoceratops	Cretaceous	Mongolia	6	Herbivorous	33
,, 4	Triceratops	Cretaceous	North America	36	Herbivorous	54
,, 4	Pachyrhinosaurus	Cretaceous	North America	16	Herbivorous	64
,, 5	Scelidosaurus	Jurassic	England	12	Herbivorous	51

CLASSIFICATION OF DINOSAURS

CLASSIFICATION		GENUS	AGE	WHERE FOUND	LENGTH (feet)	DIET	PAGE
Dinosauria	5	Kentrosaurus	Jurassic	Tanzania	15	Herbivorous	45
,,	5	Stegosaurus	Jurassic	North America	29	Herbivorous	53
,,	6	Acanthopholis	Cretaceous	Europe	13	Herbivorous	39
,,	6	Polacanthus	Cretaceous	England	15	Herbivorous	39
,,	6	Nodosaurus	Cretaceous	North America	16	Herbivorous	39
,,	6	Scolosaurus	Cretaceous	North America	19	Herbivorous	41
,,	6	Palaeoscincus	Cretaceous	North America	16	Herbivorous	40
,,	6	Euoplocephalus	Cretaceous	North America	16	Herbivorous	41
,,	7	Compsognathus	Jurassic	Germany	1-2	Carnivorous	15
,,	7	Podokesaurus	Triassic	North America	3	Carnivorous	14
,,	7	Coelophysis	Triassic	North America	6-10	Carnivorous	27
,,	7	Ornithomimus	Cretaceous	North America and Asia	12	Omnivorous	25
,,	7	Struthiomimus	Cretaceous	North America	12	Herbivorous	67
,,	7	Ornitholestes	Jurassic	North America	6	Carnivorous	28
,,	8	Velociraptor	Cretaceous	Mongolia	9	Carnivorous	26
,,	8	Stenonychosaurus	Cretaceous	Canada	6	Carnivorous	28
,,	8	Deinonychus	Cretaceous	North America	6-10	Carnivorous	29
,,	8	Gallimimus	Cretaceous	Mongolia	13	Carnivorous	31
,,	8	Dromaeosaurus	Cretaceous	North America	5-12	Carnivorous	31
,,	8	Microvenator	Cretaceous	North America	4	Carnivorous	14
,,	9	Ceratosaurus	Jurassic	North America	18	Carnivorous	58
,,	9	Spinosaurus	Cretaceous	Egypt	39	Carnivorous	56
,,	9	Tyrannosaurus	Cretaceous	North America	40	Carnivorous	56
,,	10	Thecodontosaurus	Triassic	Europe, North America	6-10	Omnivorous	10
,,	10	Plateosaurus	Triassic	Europe	19	Herbivorous	46
,,	10	Anchisaurus	Triassic	North America	8	Omnivorous	46
,,	10	Riojasaurus	Triassic	Argentina	24	Herbivorous	44
,,	10	Massospondylus	Triassic	South Africa	13	Omnivorous	67
,,	11	Dicraeosaurus	Jurassic	East Africa	42	Herbivorous	59
,,	11	Camarasaurus	Jurassic	North America	65	Herbivorous	63
,,	11	Apatosaurus	Jurassic	North America	65	Herbivorous	62
,,	11	Brachiosaurus	Jurassic	North America, East Africa	70	Herbivorous	64
,,	11	Diplodocus	Jurassic	North America	85	Herbivorous	63
Pterosauria	1	Sordes	Triassic	USSR	2*	Omnivorous	21
,,	1	Anurognathus	Jurassic	Europe	1½*	Piscivorous	21
,,	2	Pterodactylus	Jurassic	Europe	⅓-1*	Carni-Piscivorous	22
,,	2	Dsungaripterus	Cretaceous	China	10*	Piscivorous	23
,,	2	Criorhynchus	Cretaceous	Europe	3*	Carnivorous	22
,,	2	Quetzalcoatlus	Cretaceous	North America	35*	Carnivorous	66
,,	2	Pteranodon	Cretaceous	North America	25*	Piscivorous	69

*Wing span

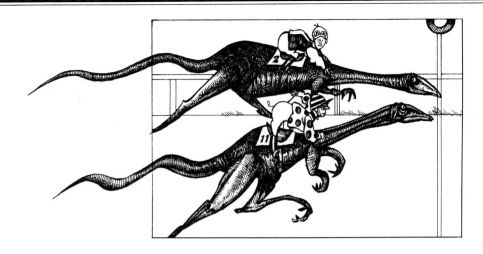

First published 1983 by
André Deutsch Limited
105 Great Russell Street London WC1

Text copyright © 1983 Robert Mash
Design copyright © 1983 Shuckburgh Reynolds Ltd

Produced, edited and designed by
Shuckburgh Reynolds Ltd,
8 Northumberland Place, London W2 5BS

ISBN 0 233 97566 7

Designed by David Fordham
Black and white illustrations by William Rushton
Colour illustrations by Diz Wallis (pages 9, 24, 49 and 68)
and Philip Hood (pages 4, 12, 17, 20, 52, 57, 60 and 65).
Typesetting by SX Composing Ltd
Colour origination by Lithospeed Ltd
Printed and bound in Spain by Printer Industria Grafica, Barcelona
DLB 20909-83